Nelson
MATHEMATICS
4
towards LEVEL 4

PUPILS' BOOK 1

Nelson

Thomas Nelson and Sons Ltd
Nelson House Mayfield Road
Walton-on-Thames Surrey
KT12 5PL UK

51 York Place
Edinburgh
EH1 3JD UK

Thomas Nelson (Hong Kong) Ltd
Toppan Building 10/F
22A Westlands Road
Quarry Bay Hong Kong

Thomas Nelson Australia
102 Dodds Street
South Melbourne
Victoria 3205
Australia

Nelson Canada
1120 Birchmount Road
Scarborough Ontario
M1K 5G4 Canada

Authors and consultants
Bill Domoney
Peter Gash
Paul Harrison
Lorely James
Ann Sawyer
Diana Wright

Contributor
Paul Broadbent

Acknowledgements

Photography
Biofotos: pages 111, 120 (left); Colorsport: pages 26, 92, 106; Greg Evans: page 110; Chris Ridgers: pages 20, 22, 32, 38, 39, 90, 105; Zefa: page 120 (right).

Design
Julia King, Thumbnail Graphics

Illustration
Jane Cheswright
Jackie East
Peter Kent
Bethan Matthews
Dave McTaggart
Helen Stanton
Stan Stevens
Nancy Sutcliffe

Produced by **AMR**

First published by Thomas Nelson & Sons Ltd 1993

ISBN 0-17-421671-8 (single copies)
ISBN 0-17-421672-6 (pack of six)
NPN 9 8 7 6 5 4 3 2

Printed in Great Britain

CONTENTS

The colour band at the foot of each page indicates the relevant section of the **Teacher's Resource File, Level 4.**

How quickly can you add?

Look at these groups of children.

Answer these questions. Try to work them out in your head.

1. How many children are skipping?

2. How many children are playing games with a ball?

3. If the tennis players joined in skipping, how many would be skipping?

4. How many children are there altogether?

5. Find four groups that can be put together to make 30.

6. Find five groups that can be put together to make 20.

7. List all the groups which could be put together to make 11.

8. How many groups of six could all the children make? Would any be left over?

Word scores

Each letter of the alphabet can be given a number score from 1 to 9.

a b c d e f g h i j k l m n o p q r s t u v w x y z
1 2 3 4 5 6 7 8 9 1 2 3 4 5 6 7 8 9 1 2 3 4 5 6 7 8

Words can be given scores.

m a t h s $4 + 1 + 2 + 8 + 1 = 16$
4 1 2 8 1

16 is the word score for maths.

1. Make three more words with a score of 16.

2. What is your name score?

3. What is your friend's name score?

4. Do longer names always have a bigger score?

5. Which has the higher score, huge or tiny

6. Do a class survey of name scores.

Ipsita turned over these cards.

| 1 | 2 | | 4 | 5 | | | 8 | |

She used these rules:
Use each card only once for each sum.
Only add numbers.

7. Can she make every number between 10 and 20?

8. How many different ways can she make 16?
   Investigate different ways of making other numbers.

There is more about addition on page 46.

Sticks and intersections

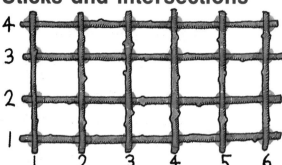

You can solve multiplication problems by laying out sticks.

This one shows 4 x 6.

There are four sticks with six sticks laid over them.
Everywhere the sticks cross there are intersections
There are 24 intersections: 4 x 6 = 24.

Draw sticks and intersections to show each of these.

1. 5 x 7

2. 8 x 8

3. 3 x 9

4. 6 x 8

5. 4 x 10

6. 8 x 9

7. 7 x 7

8. 9 x 5

9. 10 x 6

---

10. **Sticks investigation**

3 x 4 sticks
12 intersections
6 squares ✔

Sticks not only make intersections.
They also make squares.

The ticks (✔) show the squares.
Use some sticks or straws.
Investigate other arrangements like 2 x 4 or 5 x 4.

Make a chart showing the arrangement of the number of intersections and the number squares.

Can you find any patterns?

Find the factors

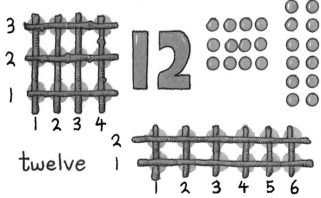

twelve

12 can be made by

6 x 2   3 x 4   12 x 1
2 x 6   4 x 3   1 x 12

Its **factors** are 1, 2, 3, 4, 6, 12

Find all the factors for each of these.

1. 36   2. 24   3. 32

4. 53   5. 30   6. 42

7. 60   8. 41   9. 35

Missing numbers

Here are parts of the multiplication square.
Copy them and fill in the spaces.

10.

5			8	
		14		18
	15			

11.

			14		
8					32
				27	
10	10				

12.

	10				30			
		24				48		

There is more about multiplication on page 48.

Hundreds, tens and ones

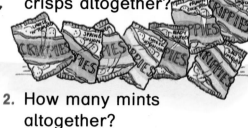

1. How many bags of crisps altogether?

2. How many mints altogether?

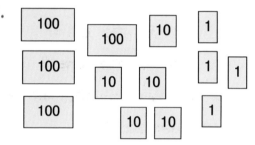
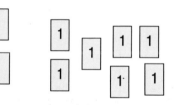

Write the numbers shown by these labels.

3.

100			
100	10	1
100		1	1
	10	10	
100		1
	10	10	

4.

100	10	10	1
10	10	10	10	1	1
	10	10	10	1	1

5.

100	1		1	1
		1		
100	1		1.	1

6.

100	100	100	1
100	100	10	10
100	100		10

Numbers can be written in **expanded** form.
This means that 627 can be written as 600 + 20 + 7.

Write these in expanded form.

7. 613

8. 226

9. 879

10. 547

11. 984

12. 732

13. 461

14. 358

Tens and riddles

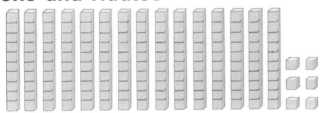

This pictures shows 156.

There are 15 tens in 156.

1. How many tens in 245?   What is left over?

2. How many tens in 652?   What is left over?

3. How many tens in 121?   What is left over?

4. How many tens in 409?   What is left over?

Some riddles

5. I have 24 tens. I am 11 away from 254. What number am I?

6. I am nearly 60 tens, but I am 9 too few. What number am I?

7. If 7 tens were added to me, I would be 400. What number am I?

8. I need 10 tens to make me 999. What number am I?

All the possibilities

Mary picked these four numeral cards.

9. Using only 3 cards at a time, what are all the possible 3-digit numbers she can make?

10. What is the biggest 3-digit number she can make?

11. What is the smallest 3-digit number she can make?

12. Choose 4 digits of your own and try this out for yourself.

Decimals on a number line

This number line is marked in tenths.

The blue arrow is pointing to 7.2.

Which numbers are these arrows pointing to?

1. red   **2.** green   **3.** yellow   **4.** orange

Draw your own number line from 3 to 5, marked in tenths.

Show these numbers.

5. 4.2   **6.** 3.6   **7.** 4.9   **8.** 3.1

Draw another number line from 21 to 24.

Show these numbers.

9. 21.5   **10.** 23.9   **11.** 22.8   **12.** 23.2

Make your own number line, marked in tenths.

Ask a friend to mark some decimals on it.

Check the answers together.

Decimal pictures

This picture shows a decimal abacus.

There are 2 tens $\longrightarrow$ 20

3 ones $\longrightarrow$ 3

6 tenths $\longrightarrow$ .6

It shows 23.6.

Write the numbers these abacus pictures show.

1.  **2.**  **3.**

4.  **5.**  **6.**

Draw abacus pictures to show these numbers.

7. 62.4 **8.** 5.5 **9.** 83.0 **10.** 20.8

---

11. **Abacus decimals investigation**

> You will need an abacus or a drawing of an abacus and some beads.

Using only 3 beads, how many different decimal numbers can you make?
Here is one possibility.

Make a list of all your numbers.

Try again using 4 beads, 5 beads, and so on.

 There is more about decimals on page 52.

Base 10 decimal pictures

This picture shows 12.3

The flat stands for 10 ⟶

The rods stand for 2

The cubes stand for .3

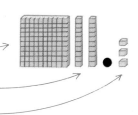

Write the numbers that these pictures show.

1.

2.

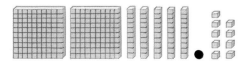

3.

4.

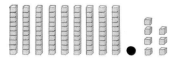

5.

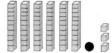

6.

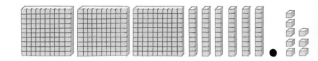

Draw pictures to show these numbers.

7. 3.6

8. 11.5

Counting in tenths

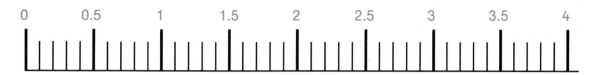

0   0.5   1   1.5   2   2.5   3   3.5   4

1. Use the number line to count in tenths from 0.7 to 1.6.
   Write all the numbers.

2. Use the number line to count back in tenths from 2 to 1.1.
   Write all the numbers.

Now do these in the same way.

3. 2.5 to 4.3   4. 0.6 to 1.9   5. 3.8 to 2.6

6. 4.0 to 2.8   7. 2.9 to 3.3   8. 2.1 to 0.9

9. **Investigating decimal divisions**

   Use your calculator.

   Write a list of numbers from 1 to 25.

   Use the calculator to divide each
   number by 10.

   Write the new numbers beside
   those you started with.

   Can you see the pattern?

   Write about it.

   Try some more numbers.

There is more about decimals on page 52.

Fractions of shapes

One half ($\frac{1}{2}$) of this circle is coloured.

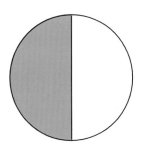

What fraction of these shapes is coloured?

1.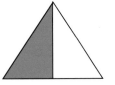

2.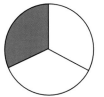

3.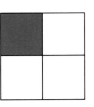

4.

5.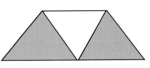

6.

7.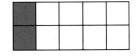

8.

9.

Each of these pictures show a quarter of a whole shape.
Draw the whole shape.

10.

11.

12.

Showing fractions

This shows $\frac{1}{4}$

You will need squared paper, scissors and coloured pencils.

Cut out strips and colour them to show these fractions.

1. $\frac{1}{2}$ 2. $\frac{3}{4}$ 3. $\frac{2}{3}$ 4. $\frac{5}{6}$

5. $\frac{4}{5}$ 6. $\frac{7}{8}$ 7. $\frac{3}{10}$ 8. $\frac{8}{9}$

9. Cut a piece of squared paper 6 x 6.

   How many different fractions
   can you show by colouring?

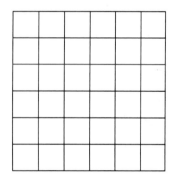

Here is one way to colour
one quarter of a square.

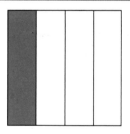

10. Find as many other ways as you can.

11. Choose a different fraction. Choose a different shape.
    Show your fraction in as many different ways as you can.

There is more about fractions on page 56.

Find the pattern

This pegboard shows a pattern made by the 3 times table.

3, 6, 9, 12, 15, 18, 21, 24, 27, 30 ..., and so on.

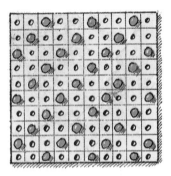

Which times tables do these pictures show?

Write all the numbers in each pattern.

1.

2.

3.

4.

5.

6.

> You will need a pegboard and some pegs or spotty paper.

7. Make a pegboard pattern for the 9 times table and draw it.

8. Investigate pegboard patterns for times tables greater than 10. For example, 11, 12, 13, 14, and so on.

   Are any similar to those below 10?

Repeating patterns

This pattern of counters is blue green red, blue green white, and then it repeats.
For quickness it can be written: b g r, b g w, b g r, b g w ...

Write these patterns in a similar way.
What is the 25th colour in each pattern?

1.

2.

3.

4.

5. Make up your own repeating pattern. Write its code. Ask your friends if they can continue it.

---

6. **How many patterns from 3 colours?**

   | You will need counters in 3 different colours. |

   How many different repeating sequences can you make from your colours?

   Here are some ideas using red, yellow, blue.

   a.  b. c.

   Write down your sequences in code.

   | There is more about patterns on page 100. |

How many ways?

All of these facts can be written about 24.

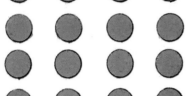

6 rows of 4 = 24

4 rows of 6 = 24

6 x 4 = 24   4 x 6 = 24

4 + 4 + 4 + 4 + 4 + 4 = 24

6 + 6 + 6 + 6 = 24

24 ÷ 4 = 6   24 ÷ 6 = 4

Do you notice that 6 x 4 makes the same as 4 x 6?

Write all the facts about these arrays.

1.

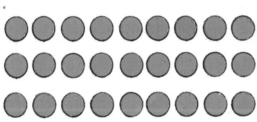

2.

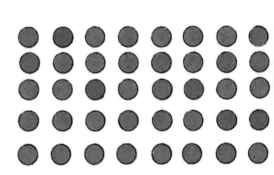

3.

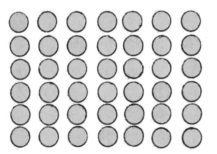

4.

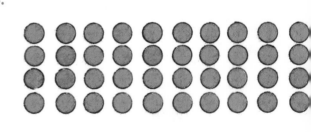

Draw these numbers as arrays and write the facts about them.

5. 32   6. 45   7. 48   8. 36

Missing operation signs

> Remember: brackets make number sentences clearer.
> Operations in brackets should always be worked
> out first.

Put in the operation signs $(+, -, \div, \times)$ to make these number sentences work. You may need to use brackets.

1. 2   3   4 = 1

2. 2 x 3   4 = 2

3. 2   3   4 = 3

4. 2 x 3   4 = 10

5. 8   3 x 2 = 22

6. 8 x 3   2 = 40

7. 8 x 3   2 = 12

8. 8   3 x 2 = 2

9. 8   3 x 2 = 10

10. 8   3   2 = 9

Number neighbours

A game for 2 players.

> You will need digit cards from 0 to 9.

Shuffle and deal the digit cards so that each player has 5.
The players lay down the digit cards in the order in which they were dealt.
To play the game, each player uses $+, -, \div, \times$ and = to make all the numbers from 1 to 10.
For example, here are 5 digit cards.

| 1 | 4 | 7 | 2 | 5 |

You can make | 1 | + | 4 | = | 5 |

| 1 | − | 4 | + | 7 | + | 2 | = | 6 |

and so on.

 There is more about number operations on page 102.

What should I use?

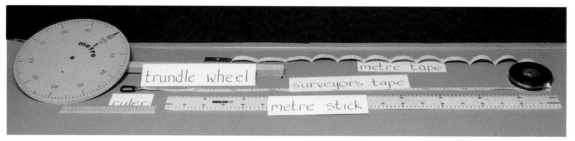

The picture shows instruments which are used to measure length.

Write what you would use to measure these, and whether you would use kilometres (km), metres (m) or centimetres (cm).

1. a netball court

2. a pencil

3. a pathway

4. the circumference of a litter bin

5. your friend's height

6. the circumference of a tree trunk

Perimeters

> Remember: the perimeter of a shape is the distance all around the outside.

Measure the perimeters of these shapes in centimetres.

7.

8.

9.

10.

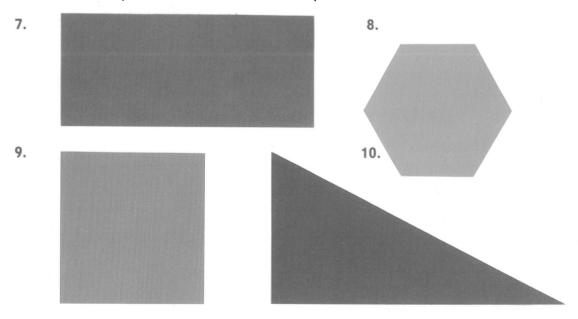

The delivery van

A van driver has to deliver to all these villages.

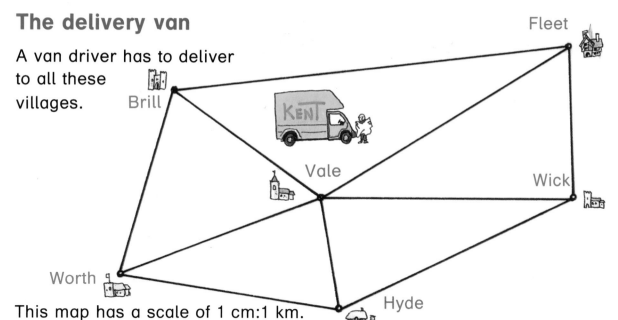

This map has a scale of 1 cm : 1 km.
The van driver starts from Fleet every day.
Use a ruler to measure the distances on the map and answer these questions.

1. On Monday he has deliveries at Wick, Vale and Worth. How long is his shortest route in kilometres?

2. What is his shortest route back to Fleet and how long is it?

3. On Tuesday he has to visit Brill and Hyde. How long is his shortest route?

4. On his return journey he has to make last minute stops at Wick and Vale. Which order should he visit them in to make the shortest trip?

5. How long is the shortest route to visit every village and return to Fleet? List the villages in order of deliveries.

Measure these. Choose what to measure with and whether to use km, m or cm.

6. The perimeter of a door.

7. The perimeter of the classroom.

8. The perimeter of the playground.

Which is best?

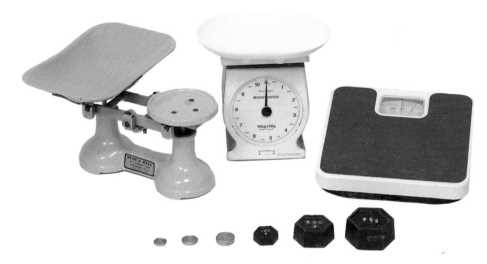

These are all used for weighing. Write down what you would use to weigh these objects. Also write down whether the result would be kg, g or kg and g.

1. your best friend

2. a pencil

3. a large bag of potatoes

4. a litre of water

5. a paperback book

6. a brick

If possible, use real things to check your answers.

Worth your weight in gold

7. How much do you weigh?

> Remember: 1kg 575 g can be written as 1.575 kg

8. What would you be worth if your weight was measured in 20p coins?

9. What would you be worth if your weight was measured in £1 coins?

> Hint: you will need to weigh a real 20p and a real £1 coin. You may wish to use a calculator to help with the working out.

How many of you would balance?

Weigh yourself in kilograms.

1. How many children like you would it take to balance a 5 tonne elephant?

2. How many children like you would it take to balance a $\frac{3}{4}$ tonne polar bear?

3. How many children like you would it take to balance a 1 tonne motor car?

Weighing water

4. Weigh 1 litre of water. Write the weight on a chart like this. Work out how much $\frac{1}{2}$ litre, 100 ml and 2 litres weigh.

   Check your answers by weighing.

Water	Weight
1 litre	?
$\frac{1}{2}$ litre	?
100 ml	?
2 litres	?

Counting cubes

> Remember: the volume of a shape is the amount of space
> it occupies.

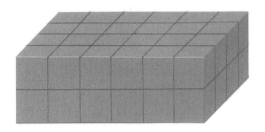

You can work out the volume of this cuboid by counting the cubes. There are 48 cubes altogether, but some of them are hidden in the picture.

The volume of this cuboid is 48 cubes.

Use interlocking cubes to make these cuboids and find their volumes.

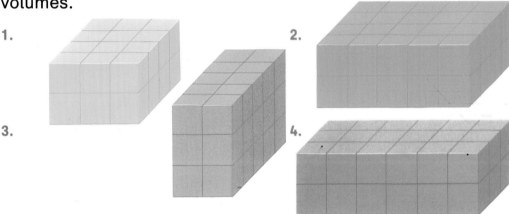

1.

2.

3.

4.

---

5. **How many cuboids?**

Here is one cuboid which can be made from just 12 cubes.

How many different cuboids can you make using just 12 cubes? What is the volume of each?

Making plans

The plan below was used to make this shape.

3	3	3
2	2	2
1	1	1

1. What is the volume of the shape?

Draw these plans on squared paper and use the cubes to build the shapes. Find the volume of each shape.

You will need squared paper and interlocking cubes.

2.

1	2	3
2	3	2
3	2	1

3.

2	2
3	3
4	4
5	5

4.

5	3	5	3

5.

1	2	3
2	3	4
3	4	5

6.

2	3	2
1	3	1

7.

5	4	
3	5	
3	4	5
2	3	3

Draw some plans of your own. Let your friends build the shapes and find the volumes.

Complete the cuboid

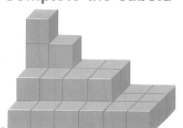

Use interlocking cubes to make this shape. Make the shape into a cuboid with the same size base and the same height by building the other half.

Make one for your friend to complete.

There is more about finding volumes on page 68.

How long did it take?

Clare began the cross-country ski
race at 09:30. She finished 4 h 21 min later.
What time did she finish?

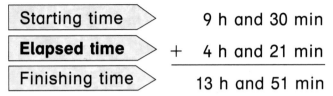

Starting time	9 h and 30 min
Elapsed time	+ 4 h and 21 min
Finishing time	13 h and 51 min

Clare finished at 13:51.

Clare's friend began the race at 09:45 and
finished at 14.57. How long was he skiing?

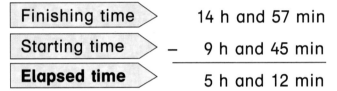

Finishing time	14 h and 57 min
Starting time	− 9 h and 45 min
Elapsed time	5 h and 12 min

He was skiing for 5 h 12 min.

1. Here is a chart of starting times, finishing times and elapsed
   times. Some of the times are missing.

   Copy the chart and fill in the missing times.

Skier	Starting time	Elapsed time	Finishing time
1.	08:20	5 h 10 min	
2.	10:05	6 h 2 min	
3.	09:13		16:20
4.	08:27		15:50

2. The race officials started work at 08:15. They worked for
   10 h 30 min. What time did they finish work?

3. Think of an activity like making a tables square, walking once
   around the playground or reading a page of your book. Make a
   chart like the one above. Time yourself and your friends.

Take a commercial break

Most commercial breaks on television last $3\frac{1}{2}$ minutes.

Look at the list of advertisements. How long will these commercial breaks last?

Advertisement	Time taken
Nissan Sunny GTI	30 secs
Dunlop Tyres	40 secs
Delmonte Fruit	10 secs
Shower Electric	30 secs
Harrods Sale	30 secs
Vodaphone Recall	40 secs
Snickers Ice-cream	30 secs
Ponds Skin Cream	20 secs
Cornflakes	30 secs
Cesar Dog Food	20 secs
Fairy Washing Powder	30 secs
P G Tips	30 secs
Stop Car Crime	40 secs

1. Shower Electric, Delmonte Fruit, Ponds Skin Cream, P G Tips, Stop Car Crime, Snickers Ice-cream, Cesar Dog Food.

2. Fairy Washing Powder, Harrods Sale, Nissan Sunny GTI, Dunlop Tyres, Cornflakes, Vodaphone Recall.

3. Use the list to make up your own commercial break lasting exactly $3\frac{1}{2}$ minutes.

   Write the advertisements and their times in the order they will appear on television.

4. **Make a boat**

   Use Plasticine or paper to make a boat that will float on the water for at least 10 seconds. Estimate, then measure the time it takes from collecting the materials to when the boat first floats. Work with a friend and compare your times with your estimate.

   There is more about time on page 106.

Areas of rectangles

Remember: area is the measurement of a surface.
The area of a rectangle can be found by multiplying length by breadth. l x b = area.

Measure these rectangles and write their areas in square centimetres.

1.

2.

3. 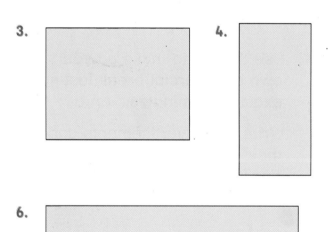   4.   5.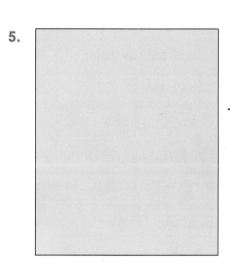

6.

7. Draw a rectangle 4 cm long and 2 cm wide.
   Write down its area. Now double the length.
   What is the new area? Try this with other rectangles.

8. Do the same as in Question 7, but this time double the length
   and the width. What happens to the area?

Areas of other shapes

This shaded area is 1 cm².
This shaded area is 0.5 cm².
This shaded area is 1 cm².

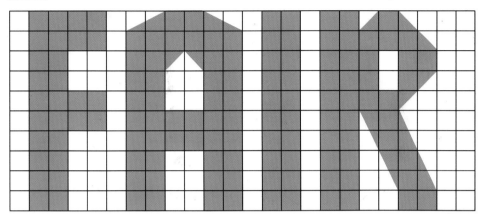

1. Write the area of each letter.

2. Write the total area covered by the whole word FAIR.

3. Write the area of paper not covered by the word FAIR.

4. Use centimetre squared paper. Write your name or initials. Work out the area of each letter and the total area covered.

Draw these shapes.

Use centimetre squared paper to draw these:

5. an L covering 6 cm²

6. a T covering 18 cm²

7. a right-angled triangle covering 4.5 cm²

8. an F covering 8 cm²

9. an irregular hexagon covering 10 cm²

10. a + sign covering 20 cm²

Try some shapes of your own and set them as puzzles for a friend.

 There is more about area on page 66.

Polygons

Remember: a polygon is a closed shape whose sides are
straight lines.

Are these polygons?

1.
2.
3.
4.

Write the names of these polygons.

5.
6.
7.
8.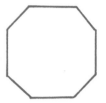

Write the names of the polygons with these features.

9. 3 vertices   10. 6 sides   11. 4 vertices   12. 5 sides

Draw a polygon with the following:

13. 6 vertices   14. 4 equal sides   15. 5 vertices   16. 3 sides

---

These are
pentagons.

These are
not pentagons.

Which of these
are pentagons?

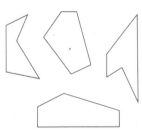

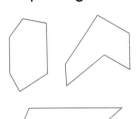

17.   18.

19.   20.   21.

Investigating polygons

Geoboard polygons

Use geoboards or spotty paper to make these polygons.
Write their names.

1.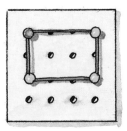

2.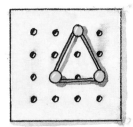

3.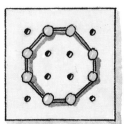

4.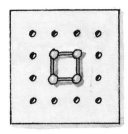

5.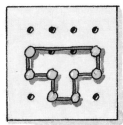

6.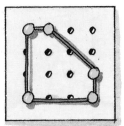

---

7. Find out what these road signs mean.
   Write what shapes they are.

Which shapes are the most common for traffic signs?

---

8. **Halving a hexagon**

   Draw a regular hexagon and cut it out.
   Draw a line or fold the hexagon to
   divide it into two halves.
   How many ways can you halve your hexagon?
   Try other shapes.

There is more about polygons on page 34.

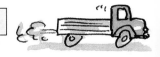

Finding right angles

 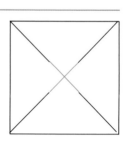
1. Find 6 right angles in this picture.
   Write down what they are.

If you draw the diagonals of a square,
there will be 4 right angles where
the diagonals cross.

Draw these shapes.

Draw diagonals. Which ones make right angles?

2.
3.
4.

5. Try other regular shapes.

6. Try irregular shapes.

Geoboard investigations

Remember: a right angle measures 90°

The shape on this geoboard
has 4 right angles and 4 sides.

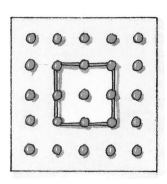

How many right angles do these shapes have?

1.

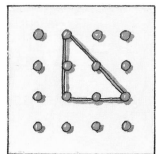

2.

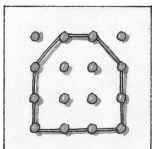

3.

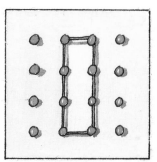

Use a geoboard or spotty paper to make these shapes.

4. a quadrilateral with
   1 right angle

5. a pentagon with 3 right
   angles

6. a hexagon with 2 right
   angles

7. a quadrilateral with
   2 right angles

8. What is the least number of sides a shape must have if it has
   2 right angles?

Investigating rectangles

> You will need different sized geoboards, elastic bands and spotty paper.

1. How many different sized squares can you make on a 9-pin geoboard?

   This picture shows one.

2. How many other rectangles can you make?

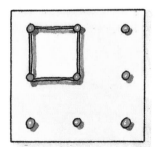

Now use a 16-pin geoboard.

3. How many different sized squares can you make?

4. How many other rectangles can you make?

5. Experiment with other geoboards.

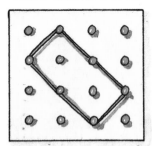

> You will need used matchsticks or craftsticks.

Make these patterns and solve the puzzles. Draw the new pattern.

6.

Remove 2 matches
to leave just 2 squares

7.

Move 3 matches
to make 4 squares

8.

Move 2 matches
to make 7 squares

Squares from rectangles

A square can be made from a rectangle of paper by folding.

rectangle   draw   fold   square

Trace these rectangles and cut them out.

Fold them to make squares.

Measure the squares and write the lengths of their sides.

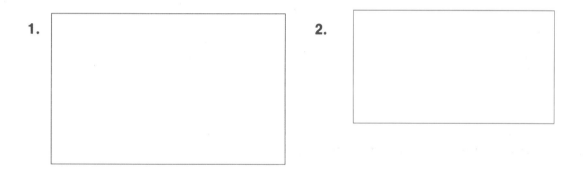

1.

2.

3.

4.

There is more about squares and rectangles on page 116.

Is it a cuboid?

Remember: a cuboid has 6 rectangular faces, right-angled vertices and the opposite faces are identical (or congruent).

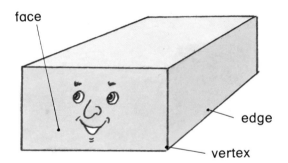

A cube is a special sort of cuboid because **all** its faces are identical.

Which of these nets will make a cube or cuboid? Draw them and try to make the shapes.

1.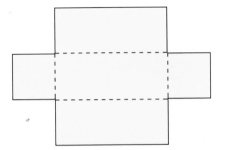

2.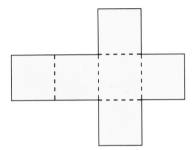

3.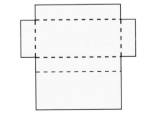

4.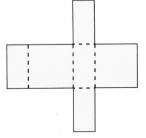

5.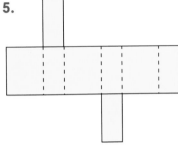

6.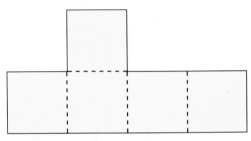

Making cubes and cuboids

This cube has edges which are 4 cm long.

It measures 4 cm x 4 cm x 4 cm

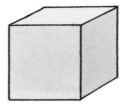

1. Draw the net for this cube and make it.

Make these cubes and cuboids in the same way.

2. 8 cm x 8 cm x 8 cm
3. 4 cm x 6 cm x 2 cm
4. 3 cm x 7 cm x 3 cm
5. 5 cm x 5 cm x 5 cm

---

6. **Matchboxes**

The inside part of a matchbox must be able to slide in and out of its cover. Make one for yourself.

Draw a net for each part.

Making dice

These are nets of dice with some of the numbers missing.
Draw them and write in the missing numbers.

7.
```
    4
5   6
```

8.
```
      4 2 3
      6
```

9.
```
        2
3   1
        5
```

10.
```
3 5
    6
```

11. Choose one of the nets and make a dice.

There is more about constructing 3-D shapes on page 118.

Getting organised

Kamaljit asked children in the class which two pieces of fruit they would like to take with them on the class picnic. To help him buy the fruit, he made this tally chart.

fruit	tally
apples	IIII IIII IIII IIII
pears	IIII IIII III
oranges	IIII IIII IIII
bananas	IIII IIII
peaches	IIII IIII
nectarines	IIII II

How many of each of these fruits would Kamaljit need to buy:

1. apples
2. pears
3. oranges
4. bananas
5. peaches
6. nectarines

7. Remember each child in the class was allowed to choose two fruits. How many children are there in Kamaljit's class?

8. Imagine your class is going on a picnic.

    Find out which two pieces of fruit each child would like to take. They may want different fruits from Kamaljit's.

    Make a tally chart.

Stocktaking

Mrs Marshall needs to know how many felt-tipped pens she has to order.

1. Make a table to show how many of each colour. Put the colours in order from most to least.

Colour	Number
?	?

2. Think of something in your school that may need sorting out. For example, PE bands, rubber balls or even felt-tipped pens. Sort them neatly and make a table to show how many of each.

There is more about tallying on page 78.

A typical day

Maria drew a graph of how she spent one school day.

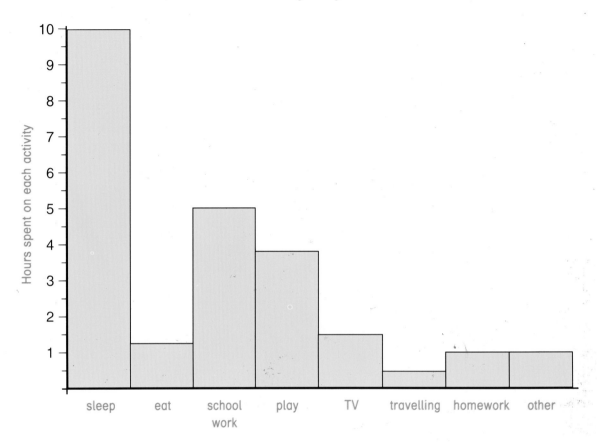

My Day

1. How long did she spend eating?

2. How long did she choose to watch TV?

3. How much time did her homework and school work take up?

4. What did she spend the longest time doing?

5. What did she spend the least time doing?

6. Make your own chart showing how long you spend on different activities during the day.

Representing and interpreting data   Unit 1   Interpreting bar charts

Check the temperature

Rajesh took the temperature every hour during the school day.

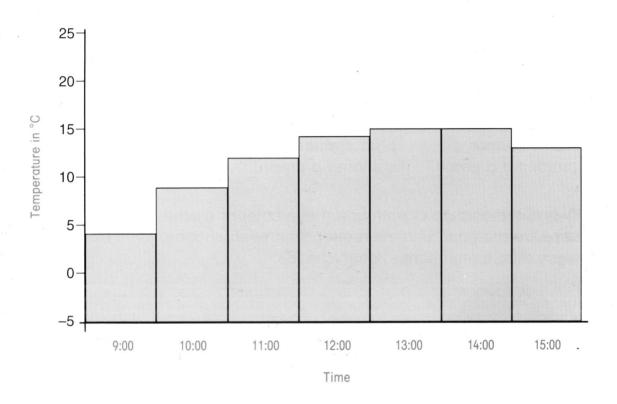

Temperatures on a Spring day

1. What was the temperature at 11:00?

2. Which was the coolest part of the day?

3. Was it warmer at 12 noon or 3 p.m?

4. What do you think the temperature might have been at 4 p.m?

5. Check the temperature at hourly intervals throughout one day. Make your own bar chart to show the information.

6. Check the temperature at 10 a.m. for 3 consecutive days. How much does it vary?

What is the chance?

 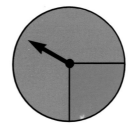 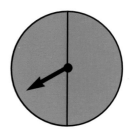

On this spinner there is a **certain chance** of spinning a red, and **no chance** of spinning a green.

On this spinner there is a **good chance** of spinning a red, and a **poor chance** of spinning a green.

On this spinner there is an **even chance** of spinning **either** a red **or** a green.

What is the chance of spinning these colours on the spinners? Use these words: good chance, better than even chance, even chance, worse than even chance, poor chance.

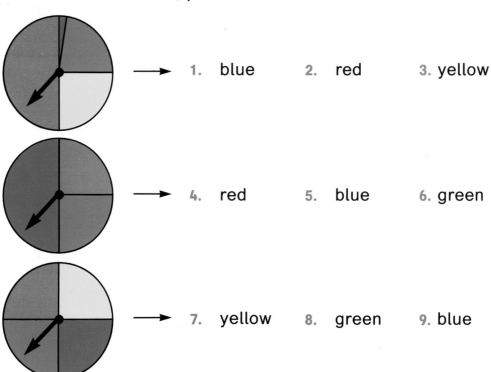

1. blue   2. red   3. yellow

4. red   5. blue   6. green

7. yellow   8. green   9. blue

Lucky or unlucky dips

In this bag of marbles there is a
good chance of pulling out a green, a
poor chance of pulling out a yellow
and no chance of pulling out a blue.

What are the chances of pulling out these.

1. red	2. blue	3. yellow

4. green	5. yellow	6. red

7. blue	8. green	9. yellow

Make and test

You will need a bag or box and different
coloured marbles or counters.

Put some different coloured marbles
in a box. Pull out one at a time and
keep a tally. Always put the marble
back before the next dip. Do it 50 times.

colour	tally
red	⊮⊮ II
yellow	III
blue	⊮⊮

10. What is the colour with the best chance of being picked?

11. What is the colour with the poorest chance of being picked?

 There is more about probability and chance on page 124.

There is more about probability and chance on page 124.

Exploring a hexagonal tangram

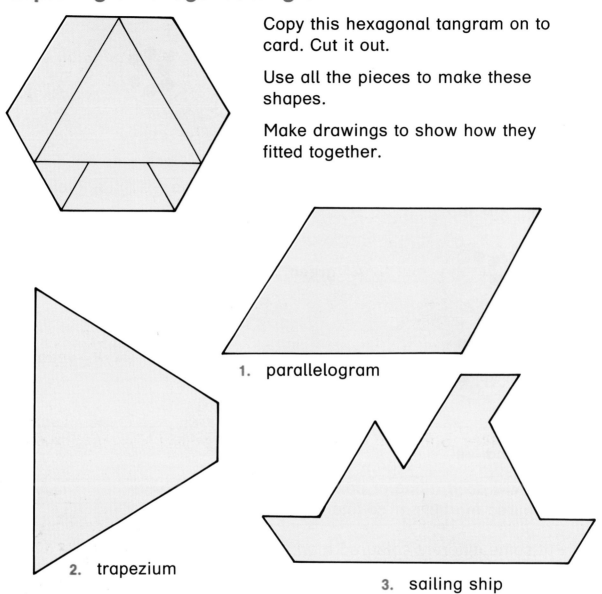

Copy this hexagonal tangram on to card. Cut it out.

Use all the pieces to make these shapes.

Make drawings to show how they fitted together.

1. parallelogram

2. trapezium

3. sailing ship

4. Use the pieces to make your own shapes and pictures.

5. Draw a hexagon like the one at the top of the page. Divide it up differently. Cut it out to make your own tangram. Try to make as many different shapes as you can.

Name them and draw them.

Tangram tiles

cut

cut

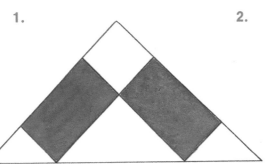

Make tangram tiles.

On a square of card, draw another square. Colour it in.

Cut the square of card diagonally to make 4 triangular tiles.

Use your tiles to make these shapes. Make drawings to show how you fitted the tiles together.

1.

2.

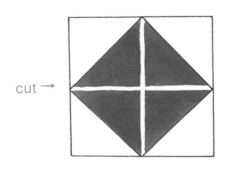

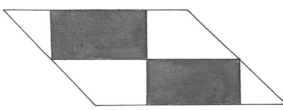

Use your tiles to make up other shapes and patterns. Keep a record of them.

↓ cut

cut →

3. Another way to make tangram tiles is to cut the card square into 4 smaller squares. Find as many different shapes and patterns as you can.

4. With some friends, use lots of square and triangular tiles to make bigger patterns.

There is more about Tangrams on page 84.

Hitting the target

39

+ 13

52

Find the missing numbers in these pictures.

Work out the answers in your head.

1. 17   + 24

2.   + 36   62

3. 37   + 48

4. 48   104

5.   + 32   91

6. 63   + 19

7.   + 27   102

8. 84   117

9. 92   + 19

10.   + 39   80

Adding and subtracting lots of numbers

1. What do all the yellow squares add up to?

2. Find 2 red squares with a difference of 41?

3. Which 3 blue squares (one from each face) add up to 85?

4. What do all the red squares add up to?

5. Which is the greater total? All the blue squares or all the yellow squares?

---

6. Put + or − into the spaces to make this true.

   1   2   3   4   5   6   7   8   =   90

   How many ways can you find?

   Use different arrangements of + and − to make other numbers.

> There is more about adding and subtracting 2-digit numbers on page 86.

What can you remember?

Harjinder has filled in all the multiplication and division facts he can remember quickly.

For example, he knows 8 x 4 = 32, 4 x 8 = 32, 32 ÷ 4 = 8, 32 ÷ 8 = 4.

X	1	2	3	4	5	6	7	8	9	10
1	1	2	3	4	5	6	7	8	9	10
2	2	4	6	8	10	12	14	16	18	20
3	3	6	9	12	15					30
4	4	8	12	16	20			32		40
5	5	10	15	20	25	30				50
6	6	12			30					60
7	7	14					49			70
8	8	16		32						80
9	9	18							81	90
10	10	20	30	40	50	60	70	80	90	100

1. Copy and complete Harjinder's tables square.

2. Make your own tables square. Write in all the multiplication and division facts you can remember quickly.

   Ask a friend to test you.

Under your thumb

7	56	8

This card has 7, 8 and 56
on it because 7 x 8 = 56.

These cards are similar but one number has been covered
by someone's thumb.

Write the missing numbers.

1. | 5 | | 9 |

2. | 4 | 36 | |

3. | | 27 | 9 |

4. | 7 | 35 | |

5. | 9 | | 7 |

6. | 8 | 56 | |

7. | | 28 | 4 |

8. | 8 | 24 | |

9. | 6 | 36 | |

10. | 7 | | 3 |

11. | 6 | 42 | |

12. | | 40 | 8 |

13. | 8 | 72 | |

14. | 8 | | 6 |

15. | 6 | | 3 |

16. | 8 | | 8 |

17. | 6 | | 9 |

18. | | 24 | 6 |

Make your own set of cards.
Use them to play a game with a friend.

There is more about multiplication on page 88.

What happens after 999?

Start at 999. Add or count on these numbers. Write the answers.

1. 1
2. 3
3. 7
4. 11
5. 22
6. 68
7. 96
8. 125

Calculator steps

Gemma started with 1235 in her calculator.

She wanted to get to 2546.

She added 100.   She added another 200.

| 1335 | | 1535 |

9. Use your calculator and write the next steps she might take to get to 2546.

Use your calculator and write the steps you would take to get from:

10. 2615 to 4273
11. 1965 to 2964
12. 5125 to 9999

Hundreds and thousands

10 hundreds = 1000

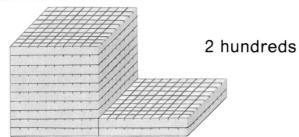

2 hundreds

Twelve hundreds make 1200.

Write these using numerals.

1. Twenty-one hundreds
2. Forty-five hundreds
3. Eleven hundreds
4. Thirty-two hundreds
5. Ninety-two hundreds
6. Sixty-three hundreds
7. Fifty-eight hundreds
8. Seventy-seven hundreds

There are twenty-three hundreds in 2357.
Write how many hundreds there are in these numbers.

9. 5792
10. 3650
11. 8275
12. 1960
13. 2489
14. 9760
15. 4257
16. 6283

---

17. **How many 4-digit numbers?**

How many different 4-digit numbers can you make with these cards?
Make some digit cards of your own.
Choose 4 and try this again.

There is more about 4-digit numbers on page 90.

Put them in order

This is a number line with the numbers missing.

A, B and C show the positions of three decimal numbers.

A is 2.5   B is 3.3   C is 4.2

Write the decimal numbers that these letters show.

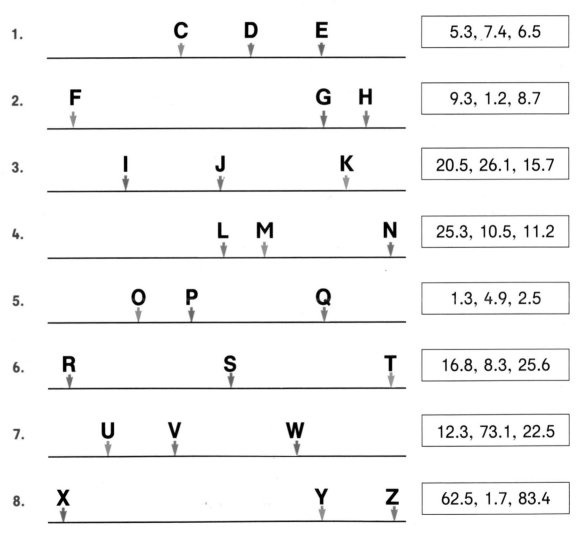

1.

      C   D   E   5.3, 7.4, 6.5

2.

F   G   H   9.3, 1.2, 8.7

3.

I   J   K   20.5, 26.1, 15.7

4.

    L   M   N   25.3, 10.5, 11.2

5.

   O   P   Q   1.3, 4.9, 2.5

6.

R   S   T   16.8, 8.3, 25.6

7.

  U   V   W   12.3, 73.1, 22.5

8.

X   Y   Z   62.5, 1.7, 83.4

Make up some of your own for a friend to try.

Greatest and least

Order these decimal numbers from greatest to least.

1. 6.8, 5.9, 7.1

2. 15.3, 20.5, 9.7, 19.7

3. 86.8, 87.9, 86.5, 87.1

4. 31.4, 59.0, 39.1, 45.2, 51.1

Order these decimal numbers from least to greatest.

5. 9.8, 4.3, 11.1, 7.4

6. 15.3, 9.4, 12.8, 10.0

7. 43.3, 39.1, 36.8, 41.0, 36.2

8. 19.9, 18.7, 19.1, 18.3, 19.6

---

9. Make your own decimal numbers.

| You will need numeral cards 0 to 9, and counters or coins. |

       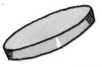

0 1 2 3 4 5 6 7 8 9

Spread out the cards face down.

Choose two. Use the counter as a decimal point.
Make the largest and smallest number you can. Write your result like this:

2 • **4** < **4** • **2**

(Remember you can use < to show less than
and > to show greater than.)

Do this ten times and write your results down.
Now use 3 cards. Make as many 2-digit decimals as you can.
Put them in order.

For example, if you chose 4, 6 and 7, you would make 4.6, 6.4
and 4.7, 7.4 and 6.7, 7.6. In order they would be:
4.6, 4.7, 6.4, 6.7, 7.4, 7.6

| There is more about decimals on page 92. |

Fruit punches and cocktails

Anita made an orange and pineapple punch for her party.
She mixed 1.5 litres of pineapple juice with 2.5 litres of
orange juice.

1.5 l + 2.5 l

She made 4.0 l of punch.

How much punch would you get from these recipes?

1. Apple and Blackcurrant Punch
   1.5 l apple juice, 0.5 l blackcurrant juice, 1.5 l lemonade

2. Mixed Fruit Cocktail
   0.3 l grape juice, 0.2 l pineapple juice, 0.4 l apple juice,
   0.5 l mineral water

3. Grape and Ginger Soda
   0.7 l grape juice, 0.5 l ginger ale, 1.2 l soda water

4. Citrus Ice-cream Fizzer
   0.6 l orange juice, 0.4 l lime juice, 0.8 l lemon squash,
   1.5 l lemonade, 0.4 l vanilla ice-cream

5. Do you know a recipe for a punch or cocktail?
   If not, make one up, using your favourite flavours, to make
   4 litres

Wheel of fortune

Kim and Simon
made a Wheel of
Fortune game.
They took turns
to spin it.

Answer these questions.

1. Kim scored 3.9. Simon scored 4.5.
   What was their total score?

2. Kim scored 5.0. Simon scored 2.3.
   What was the difference between their scores?

3. Kim scored a yellow, a blue and a pink.
   What was her total score?

4. Simon scored a purple, and 2 blues.
   What was his total score?

5. Which would give you the highest score, 2 blues and a red
   or 2 reds and a blue?

6. What is the difference between scoring a brown and an orange?

7. Make your own wheel of fortune. Use a drawing pin or
   paper fastener for the spinner. Write your own decimal numbers
   on it. Play it with a friend. Invent your own rules.

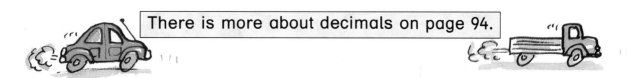

There is more about decimals on page 94.

Fractions of a set

1. What fraction of the children have black hair?
2. What fraction of the group have red tops?
3. What fraction of the children are girls?
4. What fraction of the girls are wearing black shoes?
5. What fraction of the whole group are wearing black shoes?
6. What fraction of the children with fair hair are wearing trousers?
7. What fraction of the children with brown hair are wearing trainers?
8. What fraction of the children are wearing shorts?
9. Make up some problems of your own about this picture. Try them on your friends.

Fractions of solid shapes

This picture shows a cube made up of smaller cubes.

Use the picture or make your own cube to help you answer these questions.

1. How many cubes are there altogether?

2. If you took one third of the cubes away, how many would be left?

3. Draw $\frac{1}{9}$ of the cubes.

4. $\frac{4}{9}$ of the cubes are in one pile. The rest are in another pile. How many cubes are there in each pile?

These cubes have been put together to make a cuboid.

5. How many cubes are there altogether?

6. What fraction of the cubes are red?

7. Draw $\frac{1}{8}$ of the blue cubes.

8. Add together $\frac{1}{4}$ of the red cubes and $\frac{1}{4}$ of the blue cubes. How many cubes do you have?

9. Put $\frac{1}{6}$ of the red cubes in a row. Put $\frac{1}{4}$ of the blue cubes in a row. Which row has more cubes?

10. Make or draw your own cuboid. Try a different size or use three colours for the bricks.

    Make up some problems for a friend.

 There is more about fractions on page 96.

How does the pattern grow?

Asif made this cross with sticks.
He wrote the number of sticks – 4.

He made it grow by adding more
sticks. He wrote the new total – 8.

He made it grow three more times.

1. Draw Asif's patterns of sticks.

2. Write down his series, 4, 8, ____ , ____ , ____ .

3. What is the pattern?

Make each of these patterns grow.

Use sticks or make drawings. Write the numbers under each shape.
How many sticks are there in the fifth shape? What is the pattern?

4.   5.   6.

You can use sticks to make other patterns.

Continue these patterns. What do you notice about the way the numbers grow?

7.   8.

Continue these shape patterns with sticks.

Write down the total number for each shape.

9.   10.

Germs

Germs increase by splitting.

You can use counters as germs.

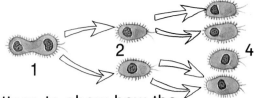

Start with one counter. Make a pattern to show how the germs continue to split.

1. Draw the pattern and write the number of germs after each split. Carry on as far as 12 splits.

2. How many germs after 5 splits?

3. How many germs after 7 splits?

4. How many germs after 10 splits?

5. What do you notice about the pattern?

Picture frames

Remember: the perimeter is the distance all around something

Paul used 1 cm cubes to make picture frames.

10   14   18

He wrote down how many cubes he used in each one.
His pattern was 10, 14, 18.

He then measured the perimeters with a ruler and found the measurements made a different pattern: 14 cm, 18 cm, 22 cm.

6. Continue Paul's pattern of picture frames until you have made 6 of them.

7. Write down the numbers in your series of cubes and perimeters.

8. How do the patterns grow?

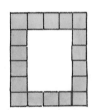

There is more about growing patterns on page 100.

Chains of numbers

Remember: you can set up a constant function on your calculator.

Numbers can grow by repeating the same number operation many times.

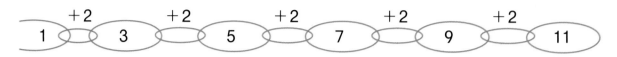

Or they can get smaller. Notice there are two operations here.

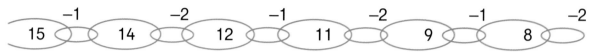

Discover the hidden operations in these chains and continue them to their 10th number.

1. 4, 7, 10, 13, 16, ...

2. 42, 38, 34, 30, 26 ...

3. 3, 4, 8, 9, 18, 19 ...

4. 2, 4, 8, 16, 32 ...

Find the longest chain

Start with a 2-digit number.   84
Multiply the two digits.   8 x 4 = 32
Multiply the two digits of the result. 3 x 2 = 6
This chain has three steps, 84 ⟶ 32 ⟶ 6

Try this with lots of 2-digit numbers.

5. What is the longest chain you can find?
6. What is the shortest chain you can find?
7. What end numbers can be made?
8. What end numbers cannot be made?

Some more number chains to investigate

Where does the chain end?

Start with any number.

If it is odd ... add 1.

If it is even ... halve it.

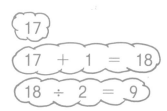

17

17 + 1 = 18

18 ÷ 2 = 9

Carry on:

9 + 1, 10 ÷ 2, 5 + 1, 6 ÷ 2, 3 → **?**

1. Where does this chain end?

2. Try lots of other starting numbers. Where do their chains end?

7 times table digits

Start with a 2-digit multiple of 7 ───────→ 28
Multiply the ones digit by 5 ─────→ 8 x 5 = 40
Add the tens digit to the result ─────→ 40 + 2 = 42
Multiply the ones digit by 5 again ─────→ 2 x 5 = 10
Add the tens digit to the result ─────→ 10 + 4 = 14
⬇
3. Continue this chain. Where does it end?   **?**
4. Try other multiples of 7. What do you notice?

Adding and squaring

Start with any 2-digit number.   25
Add the digits.   2 + 5 = 7
Square the result.   7 x 7 = 49
⬇
5. Carry on with this chain. What happens?   **?**

6. Try this with lots of different 2-digit starting numbers.
   What happens in each sequence?

There are more number chains on page 103

Measuring with centimetres and millimetres

Using millimetres on a ruler helps to measure a little more accurately.

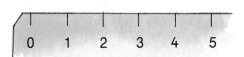

This line is 5 cm
to the nearest cm.

Using a more accurate ruler
the line is about 5 cm 3 mm long.
It is 5 cm 3 mm to the nearest
millimetre.

5 cm 3 mm can be written as 5.3 cm.

Measure these lines to the nearest millimetre.
Write their measurements in two ways.

1.   2.   3.   4.

5.

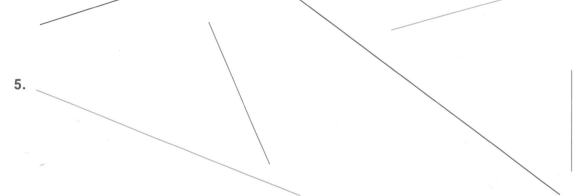

Measure each side of these shapes to the nearest millimetre.
Calculate the perimeters of the shapes.

7.    8.    9.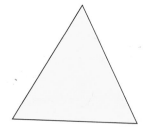

Diagonals

Remember: a diagonal is a line which joins two corners of a polygon.

diagonal

Draw these rectangles and squares. Draw the diagonals and write their measurements to the nearest millimetre.

1.

2.

3.

4.

5.

Curve drawing patterns

If you divide the lines using mm, you can make much finer curve drawing patterns.

10 9 8 7 6 5 4 3 2 1

1 2 3 4 5 6 7 8 9 10

5 mm divisions

3 mm divisions

6. Try the curve drawing pattern above. Use your own colours.

7. Design your own curve drawing pattern. Remember that each line should have the same number of points.

There is more about measuring in millimetres on page 104.

Pints, quarts and gallons

In Britain people used to measure all liquids with these Imperial measures. Some liquids are still measured in this way.

Pint (pt)   There are 2 pts in a quart.

Quart (qt)   There are 4 qts in a gallon.

Gallon (gal)

Children used to have to work out problems like these.
Try them yourself.

1. How many pints in 4 gallons?

2. How many quarts can be made from 20 pints?

3. How many quarts in 15 gallons?

4. How many pints in $6\frac{1}{2}$ gallons?

5. How many pints in $8\frac{1}{2}$ quarts?

6. How many pints altogether in 7 gallons, 3 quarts, 1 pint?

The milkman

Milkmen often deliver milk in pint bottles.

The bottles are carried in crates on the back of the milk float.
There are 20 bottles in a crate.

7. On Monday, the milkman loaded 35 crates.
   How many gallons of milk was he carrying?

8. On Tuesday, he needed to deliver 780 pints.
   How many crates did he need to load?

9. At a café, he left $2\frac{1}{2}$ crates.
   How much milk did he leave?

Bathtime

Children used to have to solve problems about filling and emptying baths. They must have been very clean!

The hot tap fills the bath with 1 pint of water every 5 seconds.
The cold tap fills the bath with 1 pint of water every 10 seconds.

Try these old-fashioned problems.

1. How long does it take to fill the bath with 8 gallons of hot water?

2. How long does it take to fill the bath with 8 gallons of cold water?

3. If both taps are running, how long does it take to fill the bath with 18 gallons?

4. When the plug is pulled out, the water drains away at 1 pint every 6 seconds. How long does it take to drain 20 gallons?

Imperial and metric

> You will need an empty pint milk bottle and a measuring cylinder marked in millimetres.

5. Fill a pint milk bottle with water.

   Pour it into a measuring cylinder marked in millilitres.

   Make a chart and write down how many millilitres in a pint. Carry on with the chart.

Imperial	Metric
1 pt	?
2 pt	?
3 pt	?

6. How many litres and millilitres in a gallon?

Complete the shape

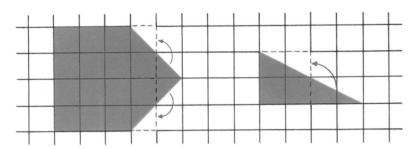

Shapes can be turned into rectangles by cutting and re-arranging.

Draw these shapes on centimetre squared paper. Cut and re-arrange them to make rectangles.

Write the areas of the new rectangles.

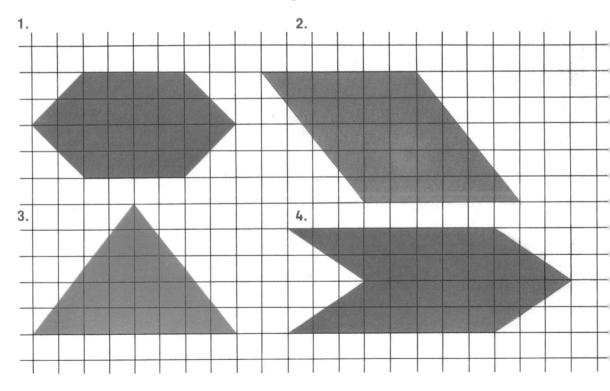

1.

2.

3.

4.

5. Draw some shapes of your own. Ask your friends to make them into rectangles. Find the areas together.

Measuring areas

Estimate, then measure to find the areas of these – in square centimetres (cm²).

1. this page
2. the table top
3. your ruler
4. a page in your reading book
5. a cupboard door
6. a window pane
7. Find something in the classroom with an area of about 600 cm².
8. Find something in the classroom with an area between 1000 cm² and 2000 cm².

Hands and feet

Estimate, then measure the area of your hand and your foot. Use squared paper.

Are the areas different?

If so, by how much.
Do the same with a few friends and compare your results.

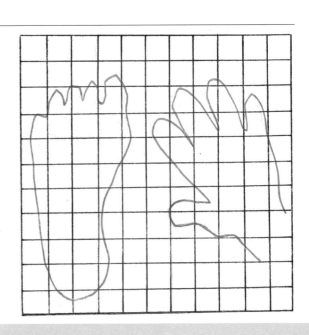

Cubic centimetres

Volume is the amount of space occupied by an object.

cm
cm
cm

The volume of each cube is one cubic centimetre (1 cm³).

What is the volume of Sean's cuboid?

Sean made the cuboid with cubes.
He has 6 cubes on the top layer.
He has 3 layers of 6 cubes.
6 x 3 = 18
The volume of Sean's cuboid is 18 cm³.

Build these shapes with centimetre cubes.
Find the volume of each. Write it in cm³.

1.
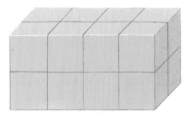

2.
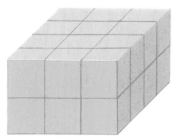

3.

4.

5.
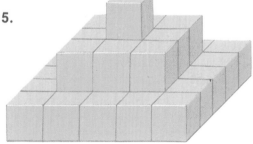

6.

Recording volumes

This chart shows how the volume of a cuboid is related to the number of cubes in each layer and the number of layers.

Number of cubes in layer	Number of layers	Volume of cuboid
12	3	36 cm³

Make a chart for these cuboids.

1.
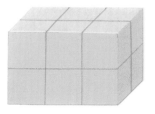

2.
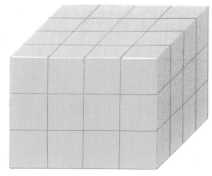

3.
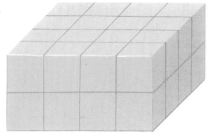

4.

Make some cuboids of your own and add them to the chart.

5.

How many blocks were needed to build the whole pyramid?

Horizontal and vertical lines

Remember: horizontal lines are level, flat lines parallel to the horizon.
The red line is horizontal.

Vertical lines are upright and at right angles to the horizon.
The yellow line is vertical.

Are these lines in the picture horizontal or vertical?

1. the red lines

2. the blue lines

3. the green lines

4. the yellow lines

5. the purple lines

6. the black lines

7. Draw your own picture showing horizontal and vertical lines.
Use one colour for horizontal and another for vertical.

8. Look around the classroom.
Find 6 horizontal and 6 vertical lines.
Write down where they are.

Treasure hunt

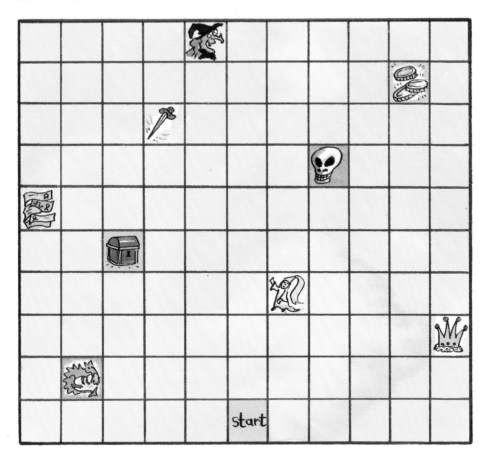

1. From the start move vertically 6 spaces up.
   Move horizontally 2 spaces right.
   What do you find?

2. From the start, move horizontally 3 spaces to the left.
   Move vertically 4 spaces up. What do you find?

3. Start at the sword. Give directions to move horizontally and
   vertically to go and kill the dragon.

4. Start from the witch. Give directions to reach the crown in
   2 moves.

5. Copy this grid. Add some more treasures and troubles.
   Make up some questions for your friends.

Parts of a circle

On this circle you can see:

an arc
a chord
a radius
a diameter
the circumference
the centre

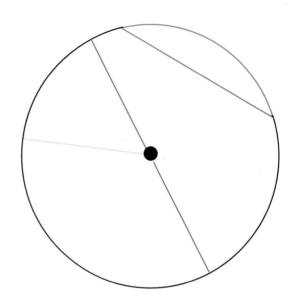

Answer these questions.

What is the name of:

1. the red line?

2. the blue line?

3. the yellow line?

4. the green line?

5. the black spot?

6. What do the black and red lines make together?

Ruler and pin investigation

You will need a drawing pin, a piece of board, a ruler, a pencil and paper.

draw a line, turn, draw a line, turn, draw a line, turn, draw a line, turn drawing, pin card

7. Describe the shape you have made.

8. Try it again with smaller turns or longer lines. Does this make a difference?

Home-made circle maker

You will need a strip of card, a drawing pin, a piece of board, a pencil and some paper.

Put a sheet of paper on the board.

Pin the strip of card, through one end, on to the centre of the paper.

Punch through the other end of the card strip with a sharp pencil.

Draw a circle. The pin will be at the centre.

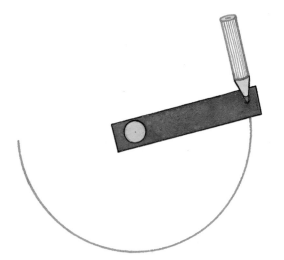

Make a circle maker which will draw circles with these radii. Draw the circles.

1. 2 cm   2. 3 cm   3. 4 cm   4. 5 cm

5. Draw a circle with a radius of 6 cm and cut it out. Mark 20 points on the circumference.

Fold each point, one at a time, into the centre.

What shape is formed by the folds?

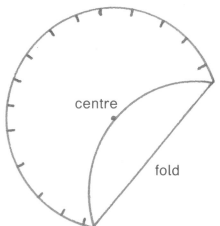

Finding your position

The picture shows how to find the point that has the ordered pair (4, 6).

Start at (0, 0).

Go 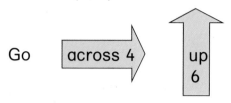 across 4   up 6

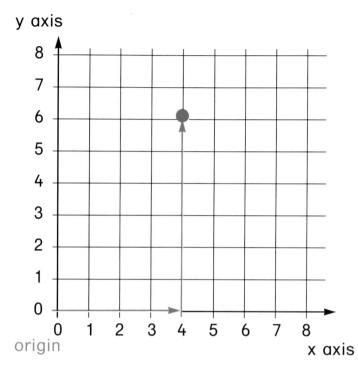

Mark the point.

Draw an 8 x 8 grid like the one above.
Make these pictures by joining the ordered pairs with lines.
Write what the pictures are.

1. START: (3,1) ➤ (1,3) ➤ (1,6) ➤ (3,8)

      (6,8) ➤ (8,6) ➤ (8,3) ➤ (6,1) ➤ (3,1) STOP

2. START: (2,1) ➤ (6,2) ➤ (7,6) ➤ (2,7) ➤ (2,1) STOP

3. START: (4,1) ➤ (1,5) ➤ (3,7) ➤ (5,7) ➤ (7,5) ➤ (4,1) STOP

4. START: (4,2) ➤ (1,2) ➤ (2,1) ➤ (6,1) ➤ (7,2) ➤ (4,2)

      (4,8) ➤ (1,3) ➤ (6,3) ➤ (4,8) STOP

5. Use a blank 8 x 8 grid. Design your own picture.
    Set the ordered pairs for a friend.

Code busters

Write the letter at these positions.
Find the answer to the riddle:
What can you serve but never eat?

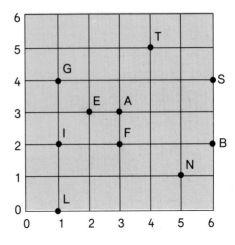

1. (3,3)   2. (4,5)   3. (2,3)   4. (5,1)

5. (5,1)   6. (1,2)   7. (6,4)   8. (6,2)

9. (3,3)   10. (1,0)   11. (1,0)

Write the letter for the ordered pair.
Find the message to answer this riddle.

I have a bank but no money.
I have branches but no leaves.
What am I?

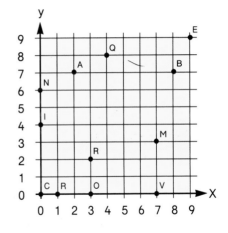

12. (2,7)   13. (3,2)   14. (0,4)

15. (7,0)   16. (9,9)   17. (1,0)

Write the ordered pair for the position of each of these letters.

18. N   19. Q   20. M   21. O   22. B   23. C

Make your own grid with letters on.
Make up a riddle or a message.
Write the ordered pairs.
Give it to a friend to try.

Treasure map

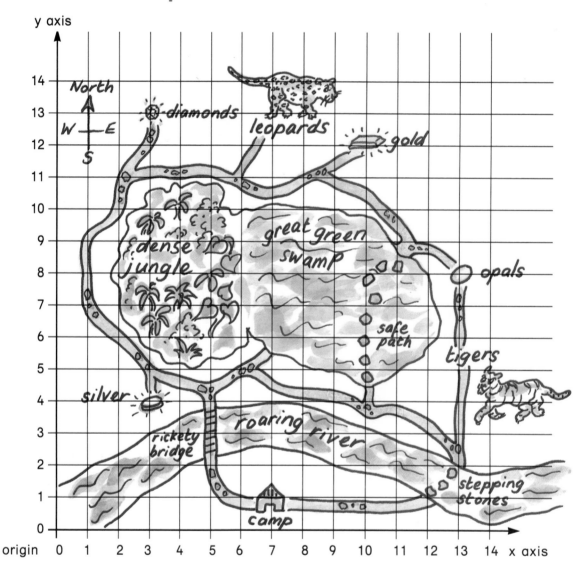

Use the map to answer these questions.

1. What would you find at (13,8)?

2. Write the ordered pairs for the location of the silver, the diamonds and the gold.

More questions on the next page ....

More map questions

3. Where does the safe path through the swamp start and finish?

4. If you went to (7,13) what danger would await you?

5. Write the ordered pairs to direct a friend from the camp to the opals. Use the stepping stones and avoid the tigers.

6. If you turned west at (10,8) where would you end up?

7. Use ordered pairs to describe the route from the diamonds back to the camp. You must use the path and the rickety bridge.

8. Find the shortest, safest route from the gold back to the camp. Write the ordered pairs for a friend to try.

9. Make your own map. Put in the co-ordinates.
   Make up some questions for a friend.

What am I?

Draw a grid with 12 points on the x axis and 9 points on the y axis.

Join the ordered pairs with lines.

START: (2,1) → (1,2) → (1,7) → (2,6) → (7,6)

(8,7) → (8,8) → (9,7) → (10,7) → (10,6)

(11,6) → (11,5) → (9,5) → (8,3) → (9,1)

(8,1) → (6,3) → (3,4) → (2,2) → (3,1) → (2,1) STOP

What have you drawn?

Sweet prices

Here are some real sweet prices.

Boost	24p	Butterscotch	£1.79	16 Flakes	99p
Mini Eggs	£1.05	Milk Tray	£2.15	3 Walnut Whips	69p
Wine Gums	86p	Toffees	89p	Roses	
Cherry Mints	49p	Aero	32p	Chocolates	£1.55
Munchies	35p	Dairy Fudge	85p	5 Chewing Gums	74p
Chocolate		All Gold	£2.39	Mini Twirls	£1.59
Brazils	£1.95	Fruit Pastilles	60p	Clearmints	72p
Black Magic	£2.35	Opal Fruits	82p	Yorkie	34p
Bassetts		Lion Bar	24p	Dime	22p
All-sorts	£2.25	Applause	47p	3 Extra Strong	
Quality Street	£1.45	Bolero	43p	Mints	73p
5 Polos	58p	Dairy Box	£2.25	3 Twix	49P
Mini Dairy Milk	£1.99				

> **Remember:** to organise lots of information it is helpful to use price ranges like 1p to 50p, 51p to £1, and so on.

1. Make a table to show which sweets' prices fall within each price range. Use:
    1p to 50p, 51p to £1, £1.01 to £1.50, £1.51 to £2, £2.01 to £2.50.

2. Which price range has most sweets in it?

    Which has least?

3. If all sweets went up by 20p, which price range would then have the most and which the least?

Car number plates

Suzanne wrote down 50 car registration numbers.

E29 AKN	D336 WMY	H658 FPH	H71 JBA
H513 GLX	C50 XDC	G456 CPK	J605 NLE
D90 APL	C237 VDD	J225 PGL	E175 HPC
C549 BUL	C555 PPG	G690 EPE	PGC 913V
B21 MPJ	E989 VGH	J501 PBH	F505 FNA
C682 FFC	YGN 190W	P177 WPK	D113 CLO
J198 SPB	A443 NUM	MYW 156D	EPG 142F
TPM 786S	A741 CPK	F629 RRX	J284 HME
B803 XHM	G106 NGT	G312 BPA	PSF 395Y
D512 OKL	G710 KGP	C157 CYW	GOY 629D
F914 HGT	C938 OFW	A503 WMG	H77 HPG
E175 HBC	H257 NOH	G693 XPB	J950 UCF
ELU 564T	H895 FVL		

1. Make a table to show how many car registrations there are in each of these number ranges.
   Use 1 to 99, 100 to 199, 200 to 299, and so on.

2. Which number range has the most in it?
   Which has the least?

3. Make your own collection of car registration numbers.
   Make a chart of the ranges.

> Remember: traffic can be dangerous – find a safe place.

Finding the mean

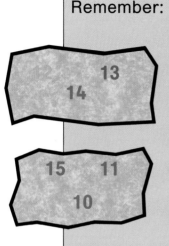

Remember: sometimes we use an average number to represent a set of numbers. For example, 12, 13 and 14 have an average of 13.

This sort of average is also called the mean.

You can calculate the mean by adding all the numbers in the set and dividing by the number in the set. For example, using 10, 11, 15;   10 + 11 + 15 = 36

There are 3 numbers,   36 ÷ 3 = 12

The mean is 12.

Find the means of these sets of numbers.

1. How many marbles can we pick up with one hand?

Name	Marbles
Paul	14
Alan	11
Katie	10
Chris	13
Ian	16
Nina	12
Bhuddi	15
Alex	12
Monique	13
Laura	14

2. How many pencils of each colour are left in stock?

Colour	Number
red	25
orange	18
yellow	14
green	22
purple	19
blue	12
pink	28
brown	16

3. Find some means of numbers in your class. For example, you could count the letters in your friends' names and find the average number of letters.

Range, mode and median

Class Name	No. in class
Mrs Jones	30
Miss Ford	27
Mr Hargreaves	28
Mrs Smith	29
Mr Heath	30
Mrs Collett	30
Miss Perry	29

The table shows class sizes in a school.

It sometimes helps to put them in order.

27, 28, 29, 29, 30, 30, 30

The range is from 27 to 30.

The mode is 30.   This is the number that occurs most often.

The median is 29.   This is the middle number when they are put in order.

Find the range, mode and median for these sets of data.

1. Newspapers delivered

SUNDAY	43
MONDAY	35
TUESDAY	35
WEDNESDAY	36
THURSDAY	37
FRIDAY	35
SATURDAY	37

2. Cans collected for recycling

JANUARY	200
FEBRUARY	300
MARCH	300
APRIL	100
MAY	300
JUNE	400
JULY	400
AUGUST	0
SEPTEMBER	300
OCTOBER	300
NOVEMBER	100
DECEMBER	100

3. Find the range of class sizes, the most common class size (mode) and the median class size for your school.

Who uses the shop?

A newsagent wanted to find out how many people used his shop in the school holidays in case he needed to order extra stock.

He counted the people who came into his shop between 12.30 p.m. and 1.30 p.m.

Here is a graph showing the results of his survey.

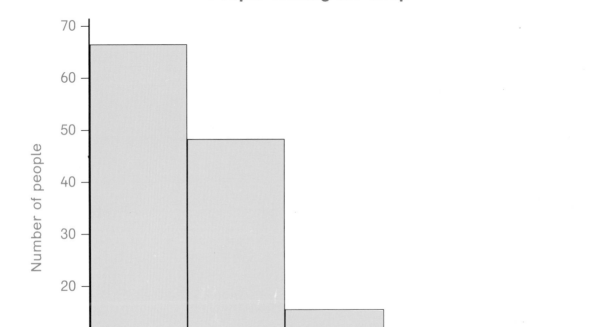

People Visiting the Shop

How many of each of these groups were there?

1. girls   2. boys   3. women   4. men   5. babies

6. How many people visited the shop altogether?

Drawing frequency diagrams

> Remember: you will need to decide on a scale for your frequency diagram. It needs to be clear enough to read easily. It must also fit the paper!

Vicky did a traffic survey to find out which was the most popular car in her area. Here are her results.

Mercedes	⊪‖ ‖‖	Ford	⊪‖ ⊪‖ ⊪‖ ⊪‖ ⊪‖ ‖
Nissan	⊪‖ ‖	Vauxhall	⊪‖ ⊪‖ ⊪‖ ‖
BMW	⊪‖	VW	⊪‖ ‖
Suzuki	‖	Rover	⊪‖ ⊪‖ ⊪‖ ‖‖‖
Fiat	‖‖	Mazda	‖
Mitsubishi	‖	Citröen	‖‖
Saab	‖	Peugeot	⊪‖ ‖‖
Toyota	‖‖‖	Renault	‖‖
Audi	‖	Volvo	⊪‖ ‖‖‖
MG	‖	Honda	‖‖‖
Jaguar	‖		

1. Use this tally chart to draw a frequency diagram of her results.

2. List the cars in order of popularity.

3. Which makes of car are most popular in your area?

   Do your own survey to find out. Draw a frequency diagram to show your results.

> Remember: traffic can be dangerous. If you are watching cars, find a safe place.

Make an egg tangram

Trace this egg tangram and transfer it to card. Cut along the lines.

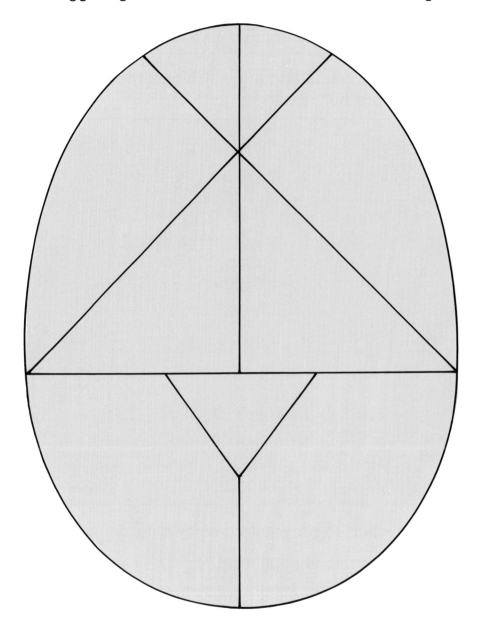

Experiment with your egg tangram to make some pictures and shapes.

Draw them and describe them.

Make these shapes

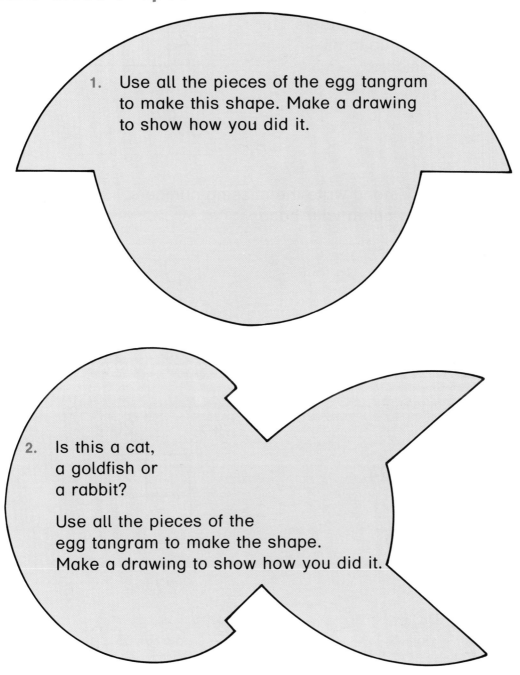

1. Use all the pieces of the egg tangram to make this shape. Make a drawing to show how you did it.

2. Is this a cat, a goldfish or a rabbit?

   Use all the pieces of the egg tangram to make the shape. Make a drawing to show how you did it.

3. Without looking at page 84, put the egg back together again. Close the book now!

Addition shapes

In this square, all the numbers in the corners add up to the number in the middle.

12		29
	122	
34		47

Draw these shapes and write the missing numbers.
Work the answers out in your head

1.

32		19
26		37

2.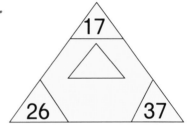

3.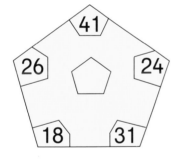

4.

45		20
	98	
		15

5.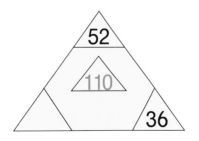

6.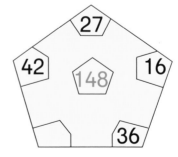

Number prisms and pyramids

1. In this triangular prism each end face is worth 25.
   Each side face is worth 36.
   What do all the faces add up to? Don't forget the hidden ones!

Add all the faces in each of these shapes.

2.

   tetrahedron

3.

   square-based pyramid

4.

   cuboid

5.

   triangular prism

A number maze

You can use
+ or – between
the numbers
in this maze.

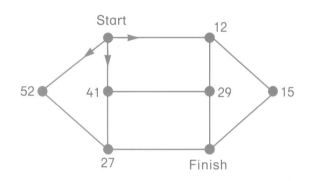

Write down routes that finish with these totals.

6. 79   7. 12   8. 9   9. 67

Table strips

This is a multiplication strip showing the 4 times table.

X	1	2	3	4	5	6	7	8	9	10
4	4	8	12	16	20	24	28	32	36	40

These tables strips have some numbers missing.
Copy them and fill in the missing numbers as quickly as you can.

1.

X	1	2	3	4	5	6	7	8	9	10
5					25					

2.

X	1	2	3	4	5	6	7	8	9	10
8								64		

3.

X	1	2	3	4	5	6	7	8	9	10
6										60

4.

X	1	2	3	4	5	6	7	8	9	10
9	9									

5.

X	1	2	3	4	5	6	7	8	9	10
7		14								

You will use these strips in the game on the opposite page.

Code breakers

This grid shows a code. To use it, you multiply two numbers to find a letter.

5 x 4 = 20
20 is the code
for V

X	6	9	7	4
5	O	W	T	V
8	E	L	M	A
3	U	S	D	I
10	N	C	P	K

1. Now break this code.

    45 48   72 3x4 40 8x6

    56 18 9x8 35 12 70 72 4x3 90 32 5x7 12 30 60

    8x4 6x10 3x7   21 12 20 12 3x9 3x4 5x6 60

Use the grid to make your own coded message.
Ask a friend to decode it.

Tables strips game

> You will need 10 counters and a stopwatch.

Each player makes a tables strip like those on page 88 with all the numbers filled in.

Decide how many numbers on the strip will be covered. The first player places counters on the strip. The other player has 10 seconds to work out which numbers are covered. He/she removes the counters from those which are correct.

The score is the number of counters collected. Swap over. Now the other player must try to collect counters.

The player with the most counters is the winner.

Putting numbers in order

Write these numbers in order from least to greatest.

1.	6125	1372	5827	3150	6324
2.	2895	3199	1596	2250	1826
3.	5643	4291	6126	5242	4871
4.	9875	8982	9645	8777	7958
5.	6708	7729	5936	6599	6821
6.	1986	2135	1520	2448	1992

Draw this number line in your book.

2000   2555   3000   4000   5000

This shows approximately where 2555 is on the number line.

Mark these numbers on your number line.

7. 3125   8. 4287   9. 4980

10. 5217   11. 1856   12. 2799

Used cars

FORD

90 (H) ESCORT 1.3 Eclipse, 1 owner, c/locking, electric front windows, Bahama blue	£5995
86 (C) ESCORT 1.6 Ghia, central locking, electric windows, 5 speed, sunroof, red	£3995
91 (H) ESCORT 1.6 LX, 1 owner, c/locking, elec/front windows, Matisse blue	£7995
88 (E) FIESTA XR2, 5 speed, sunroof, alloys, Mercury grey	£4495
88 (F) SAPPHIRE 1.8 L, blue	£5295
88 (F) SIERRA 1.6 L, 1 owner, Tasman blue	£4795
88 (E) SIERRA 2.0 GL Auto Estate, sunroof, c/locking, finished in Mercury grey	£4995
88 (E) SIERRA 2.0i Ghia, 1 owner, sunroof, electric windows, central locking, pas., radio/cassette, tinted glass, Tasman blue	£5995
87 (E) FIESTA 1.1L, split rear seat, radio/cassette, Maritime blue	£3695

OTHERS

88 (F) LADA 1.6 SLX, 1 owner, 5 speed, beige	£1995
86 (C) MINI 1000 City E, red	£2295
87 (E) MONTEGO 1. 3, 4-dr, beige	£3295
88 (F) MINI Mayfair, sunroof, 1 owner, finished in metallic blue	£3695
89 (F) VW Polo 1.0 Fox Coupe, red	£4495
88 (F) NOVA 1.2 L, 5-dr, white	£4695
88 (E) RENAULT 21 GTX, 4-dr, auto, c/locking, electric windows, electric sunroof, metallic blue	£3995

90 (G) CITROEN 14 TZS, 5-dr, e/windows, c/locking, 1 owner, black	£5695
89 (F) BELMONT 1.6L, 1 owner, blue	£4995
88 (C) FIAT Uno 60, 5-dr, beige	£1995

AUTOMATICS

87 (E) SIERRA 1.8L Auto, 1 owner, ivory	£4295
88 (F) SAPPHIRE 2.0 GL Auto, c/locking, elec front windows, 1 owner, Burgundy red	£5995
90 (H) ORION 1.4L Auto, 1 owner, Maritime blue	£5995
88 (E) SIERRA 2.0L, sunroof, c/locking, finished in Mercury grey	£4895
88 (E) CITROEN BX 19 TRS Estate Auto, in silver	£4995
90 (G) PEUGEOT 405 1.6 GL Auto, pas, sunroof, white	£6995
88 (E) RENAULT 21 GTX, 4-dr, auto, c/locking, electric windows, electric s/roof, metallic blue	£3995

PART EXCHANGES

89 (G) PEUGEOT 405 1.9 GL, pas, elec/s/roof, white	£4995
86 (C) MAESTRO 1.6L,	£2495
82 (Y) CAPRI 1600 Calypso, 2-tone Crystal green/silver	£1995
87 (D) SIERRA 2.8i 4x4 Ghia Estate, Radiant red	£4595
84 (B) ESCORT 1.3L, 3-dr radio/cassette, rear spoiler, ceramic blue	£1995

1. There are 6 SIERRAS advertised. List them in order, starting with the cheapest.

2. Which is most expensive?
   The 88 FIESTA XR2, the 88 CITROEN BX19 or the 88 NOVA 1.2L?

3. List all the ESCORTS in order, starting with the most expensive.

4. Which is cheaper?
   The 90 CITROEN 14 TZS or the 90 ESCORT 1.3 Eclipse.

5. Which car would you buy if you had £5000?

Gold, silver or bronze

Here are the points scored by competitors in different swimming events. Write the names of the people or countries who won gold, silver and bronze medals.

1.

Diving (highest score wins)	
L. Slater	108.9 points
F. Lovering	102.3 points
P. Nash	110.5 points
B. Karanov	107.5 points
F. Schultz	103.6 points

2.

100m Breast-stroke – men (shortest time wins)	
J. Warnakov	56.2 secs
D. Young	55.7 secs
P. Bermann	55.2 secs
K. Brodinski	56.9 secs
A. Holmes	58.8 secs

3.

200m Medley Relay – women (shortest time wins)	
USA	2 min 5.8 secs
CAN	2 min 6.2 secs
FRA	2 min 5.9 secs
AUS	2 min 5.6 secs
UK	2 min 6.1 secs

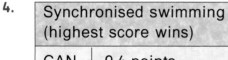

4.

Synchronised swimming (highest score wins)	
CAN	9.4 points
USA	8.8 points
UK	9.6 points
FRA	8.6 points
GER	9.3 points

Decimal maze

Scottie the dog wants to find his way home. He must always move to a space with a smaller number than the one he is on. He can move up, down, left or right only. His starting point is 9.8.

9.8	9.7	7.3
8.8	9.2	9.3	8.1
7.5	4.2	9.5	4.0
6.8	4.8	4.2	6.7
5.4	5.0	3.2	4.5
4.3	5.9	2.8	

1. How many different routes can you find for Scottie to follow?

2. What is his shortest route home?

3. Make your own decimal maze for a friend to try. You could use a route moving to larger numbers only.

Decimal addition and subtraction grids

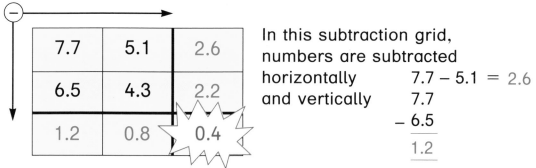

In this subtraction grid, numbers are subtracted
horizontally $7.7 - 5.1 = 2.6$
and vertically

$$\begin{array}{r} 7.7 \\ -\ 6.5 \\ \hline 1.2 \end{array}$$

0.4 is the result of all the subtractions.

Here are some addition and subtraction grids to complete. Be careful with the signs.

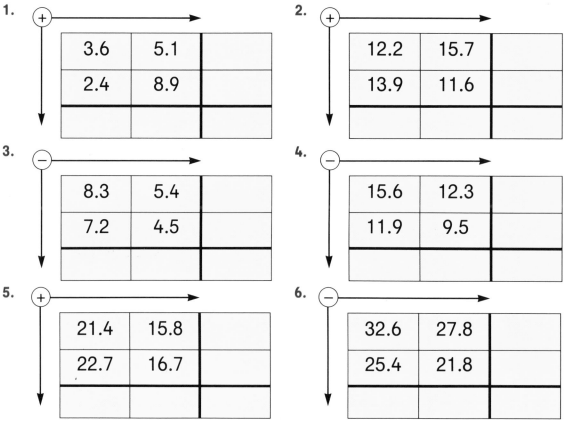

7. Make up an addition and a subtraction grid of your own.
   Try it out on a friend. Check answers together with a calculator.

Magic squares

Remember, in a magic square each row, each column and each diagonal add up to the same number.
Fill in the missing numbers in these squares.

1.

	0.9	
1.1	0.6	0.1
		1.0

2.

		4.3
	4.2	
4.1		4.6

3.

9.4		
10.3		9.3
9.7		

4.

	24.6	
24.4	24.0	25.4

5. Make your own magic square for a friend to try.

---

6. Forgetful Frances is telling a pen pal about herself.
She has forgotten to put in the decimal points. Copy the
numbers and place the decimal points for her.

Dear Clara,
My name is Frances.
I am 95 years old.
I am 1368 cm tall and
weigh 314 kg.
My brother Tom is 60
years old. He is 1000 cm
tall and weighs 245 kg.

Find the equivalent fractions

These pictures show equivalent (equal) fractions.

$\frac{1}{2} = \frac{3}{6}$

$\frac{2}{3} = \frac{6}{9}$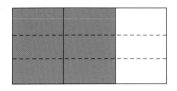

Write the equivalent fractions shown in these pictures.

1.

2.

3.

4.

5.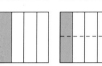

6.

Write two equivalent fractions.

7.

8.

9.

Draw a picture to show the equivalent fractions.

10. $\frac{1}{2} = \frac{2}{4}$

11. $\frac{3}{5} = \frac{6}{10}$

12. $\frac{2}{3} = \frac{8}{12}$

Use the number lines to complete the equivalent fractions.

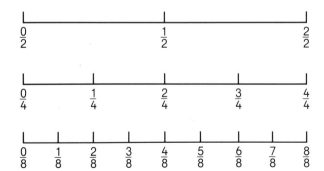

13. $\frac{1}{4} = \frac{\square}{8}$

14. $\frac{1}{2} = \frac{\square}{4}$

15. $\frac{6}{8} = \frac{\square}{4}$

16. $\frac{8}{8} = \frac{\square}{4} = \frac{\square}{\square}$

Fraction function machines

This picture shows $\frac{2}{3}$ or $\frac{4}{6}$.
If you multiply the numerator and denominator of $\frac{2}{3}$ by 2,
you get $\frac{4}{6}$. These are equivalent fractions.

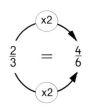

Write the equivalent fractions.

1.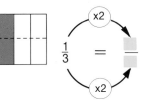

2.

3.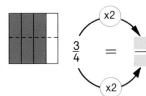

4.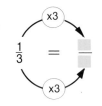

5.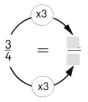

6.

7.

Halve these fractions to find the equivalent fractions.

8.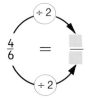

9.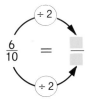

10.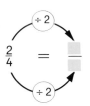

11.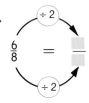

12. Cut out some 4 x 4 pieces of squared paper.

    How many equivalent fractions can you find?

    Show them by colouring the squares.

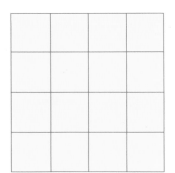

There is more about equivalent fractions on page 98.

Greater or less?

Use > or < or = to make a true statement

1.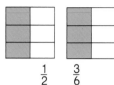

$\frac{1}{2}$ $\frac{3}{6}$

2.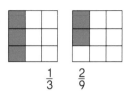

$\frac{1}{3}$ $\frac{2}{9}$

3.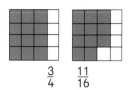

$\frac{3}{4}$ $\frac{11}{16}$

4.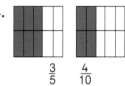

$\frac{3}{5}$ $\frac{4}{10}$

5.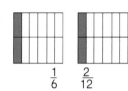

$\frac{1}{6}$ $\frac{2}{12}$

6.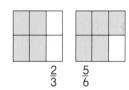

$\frac{2}{3}$ $\frac{5}{6}$

Draw pictures to help you compare these fractions.
Use >, < or = to make a true statement.

7. $\frac{1}{5}$ $\frac{3}{10}$

8. $\frac{1}{4}$ $\frac{2}{8}$

9. $\frac{5}{6}$ $\frac{9}{12}$

10. $\frac{4}{10}$ $\frac{1}{2}$

11. $\frac{2}{3}$ $\frac{5}{9}$

12. $\frac{4}{12}$ $\frac{1}{4}$

13. Two farmers have fields the same size. One plants $\frac{1}{2}$ of his with corn.

The other plants $\frac{3}{8}$ of his with corn.

Do they plant the same amount of corn?

14. Mary and Umesh have books the same length. Mary has read $\frac{3}{6}$ of hers and Umesh has read $\frac{6}{12}$ of his.

Have they read the same amount?

15. Jack and Hohy each had a mini pizza. Jack ate $\frac{5}{8}$ of his. Hohy ate $\frac{3}{4}$ of hers. Who ate more?

16. Sara may have either $\frac{1}{3}$ or $\frac{3}{9}$ of a bottle of lemonade. She likes lemonade. Which should she choose?

Put them in order

Put these fractions in order from least to greatest.
You could draw pictures to help you.

1.
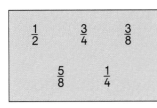

$\frac{1}{2}$ $\frac{3}{4}$ $\frac{3}{8}$

$\frac{5}{8}$ $\frac{1}{4}$

2.
$\frac{2}{3}$ $\frac{5}{12}$ $\frac{5}{6}$

$\frac{3}{6}$ $\frac{1}{3}$

3.
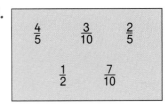

$\frac{4}{5}$ $\frac{3}{10}$ $\frac{2}{5}$

$\frac{1}{2}$ $\frac{7}{10}$

Put these fractions in order from greatest to least.

4.

$\frac{1}{4}$ $\frac{5}{16}$ $\frac{5}{8}$

$\frac{3}{4}$ $\frac{1}{2}$

5.

$\frac{7}{20}$ $\frac{3}{10}$ $\frac{1}{5}$

$\frac{3}{5}$ $\frac{9}{10}$

6.

$\frac{1}{3}$ $\frac{3}{12}$ $\frac{3}{4}$

$\frac{10}{12}$ $\frac{1}{2}$

7. When you have put all the fractions in order, add another fraction to the beginning and another to the end of each set.

Make sure they are still in order.

---

8. Make two copies of each circle. On one copy, colour 1 part of the circle. On the other, colour 2 parts. Under each circle write the fraction for the coloured part.

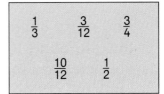

Arrange the circles in order from least to greatest, according to how much is coloured.

Patterns with cubes

You will need some centimetre cubes.

Remember: volume is the amount of space something occupies.
1cm³ means one cubic centimetre.

cube

The volume of this cube is 1 cm³. Its surface area is 6 cm².

cuboid

If you add another cube, the volume is 2 cm³. The surface area is 10 cm².

1. Add more cubes, one at a time.
   Make a chart to show the number of cubes, the volume and the surface area for each cuboid.
   Look for patterns in the numbers.
   How do the patterns grow?

More cuboids

Carry on growing these cuboids. Keep a chart. Describe any patterns you find.

2.

3.

4. Try to extend the number of patterns.
   Write down the series.
   What will be the 6th number in each series?

Diagonal cuts

You will need squared paper.

These rectangles have been drawn on squared paper. Notice how the rectangles grow.

1 x 2
2 squares cut
1 line cut

2 x 3
4 squares cut
3 lines cut

3 x 4
6 squares cut
5 lines cut

The diagonals of these rectangles cut across some squares and some lines.
You can show what happens on a chart like this.

Rectangle	Number of squares cut	Number of lines cut
1 x 2	2	1
2 x 3	4	3
3 x 4	6	5

1. Use squared paper to carry on with this series of rectangles.
   Make your own chart to show what happens.
   Describe any patterns you find.

2. Make up your own series of rectangles.
   You could try 2 x 4, 3 x 5, 4 x 6 or 3 x 6, 4 x 7, 5 x 8.

3. What happens with squares (1 x 1, 2 x 2, 3 x 3 ...)?

Calculator check

Remember: You can check the answer to a multiplication by using its inverse operation.

The inverse operation for multiplication is division.

Is this correct? 63 x 24 = 1512

Check by dividing: 1512 ÷ 24 = 63

Check these multiplications by dividing. Use your calculator. Write **correct** or **incorrect**.

1. 52 x 35 = 1820

2. 67 x 18 = 1256

3. 27 x 49 = 1423

4. 42 x 28 = 1176

5. 48 x 37 = 1776

6. 39 x 56 = 2254

Make some multiplications for a friend to check. Put in some with deliberately wrong answers.

7. **Four fours are ...**

Make all the numbers from 1 to 10 but only use fours. You can use +, −, x, ÷ , = and brackets.

Here are two ideas for making 1 and 2.

$$4 ÷ 4 = 1$$

$$(4 + 4) ÷ 4 = 2$$

If you want to make it harder, try using exactly four fours each time. For example, (4 + 4 − 4) ÷ 4 = 1

Negative numbers in chains

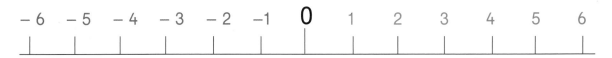

$-6 \quad -5 \quad -4 \quad -3 \quad -2 \quad -1 \quad 0 \quad 1 \quad 2 \quad 3 \quad 4 \quad 5 \quad 6$

Negative numbers   Positive numbers

You may wish to use a calculator to help with this number chain.

	key presses	display
Put a negative number into the calculator display.	− 7 =	7.−
If it is odd, subtract 3.	− 3 =	10.−
If it is even, halve it.	÷ 2 =	5.−
If it is odd, subtract 3.	− 3 =	8.−
If it is even, halve it.	÷ 2 =	4.−

1. Continue with this chain. What happens?

2. Try other negative numbers with this chain.
   What happens?

---

3. **Decimals and square roots**

   Remember: the square root key on
           your calculator looks like this √‾

   Put any number into your calculator.   20 | 20 |
   Press the √‾ (square root key) once.
   Write down the number in the display.   √‾   4.4721359
   It might be a decimal number.   √‾   2.1147425
      √‾   1.4542154
   Keep pressing the square root key.   √‾   1.2059085
      √‾   1.0981386
   Where does the chain appear to be leading?   √‾   1.047021

A maze in millimetres

Remember: there are 10 mm in 1 cm.

Here is a maze. It is drawn
using millimetres.

1. Draw the maze again, but for every mm use 1 cm.

2. Use chalk and a metre ruler. Draw the maze again on the
   playground, but for every mm use 1 m.

3. Draw your own mini-maze in millimetres.
   Enlarge it to centimetres and metres.

These sentences are written without the units km, cm, mm.

Write them again, but put in the sensible units.

4. At 11 years old, Sarah was 142   tall.

5. After driving for 68   , Marcel reached Paris.

6. When she had sharpened her pencil, the point was 5   long.

7. She needed another 10   strip of card to finish her model.

Coins

If you can, use real coins. If not, use the pictures.

Measure these to the nearest millimetre.

1. The diameter of a 5p piece.
2. The length of one edge of a 50p piece.
3. The diameter of a 1p piece.
4. The length of one edge of a 20p piece.
5. The diameter of a 2p piece.
6. The diameter of a 10p piece.
7. The circumference of a £1 coin.

If you have real coins:

8. How thick is the £1 coin?
9. How thick is the 5p coin?
10. How thick is the 50p coin?

More coin investigations   You will need real coins.

Make a chart of information about each coin.

Measure the circumference, the diameter, the thickness, and the weight.

There is more about weight on page 22.

Races and records

Keith Young (GBR)	48.1
John Masamba (UGA)	47.8
Michael Lewis (USA)	47.6
Boris Burghardt (GER)	48.7
Ralph Bell (USA)	47.7
Trevor Williamson (USA)	47.1

This is the result of a men's 400 metres hurdles race.

1. Put the race times in order from slowest to fastest.

2. Who would have won gold, silver and bronze medals?

3. Who finished in fifth place?

4. Who finished between Michael Lewis (USA) and Keith Young (GBR)?

5. Who took 1.1 seconds longer than Michael Lewis?

Timing falling paper

> You will need sheets of paper and a stopwatch which times to $\frac{1}{10}$ second.

With a partner, time how long it takes an A4 piece of paper to float to the ground. One person holds the paper horizontally 2 metres above the ground. The other person times its fall.

Do this 5 times and find the average time it takes to fall. Try tissue paper, tracing paper and card. Compare the times.

Olympic records

Women

Time	Set By	Date	Event
10.6	Florence Griffith-Joyner (USA)	1988	100m
21.3	Florence Griffith-Joyner (USA)	1988	200m
48.6	Olga Brzygina (USA)	1988	400m
1:53.4	Nadyezda Olizarenko (URS)	1980	800m
3:53.9	Paula Ivan (ROM)	1988	1500m
31:05.2	Olga Bondarenko (URS)	1988	10 000m

Men

Time	Set by	Date	Event
9.9	Carl Lewis (USA)	1988	100m
19.7	Mike Marsh (USA)	1992	200m
43.5	Quincy Watts (USA)	1992	400m
1:43.0	Joaquim Cruz (BRA)	1984	800m
3:32.5	Sebastian Coe(GBR)	1984	1500m
27:21.4	Brahim Boutayeb (MAR)	1988	10 000m

Use the information to answer these questions.

1. How much faster is the men's record for 100 m than the women's record?

2. Does it take twice as long to run 400 m as 200 m? (Check the men's and women's times.)

3. How much longer does it take a woman to run 1500 m than 800 m?

4. If Quincy Watts could run the 800 m in twice his 400 m time, would he break Joaquim Cruz's record?

5. Estimate Olga Bondarenko's 5000 m time during her 10 000 m race.

6. How long do you think it takes Florence Griffith-Joyner to run 50 m?

Reading a thermometer in °C

Remember: °C means
'degrees Celsius'
or 'degrees
Centigrade'.

0°C is the temperature at which
water freezes and 100°C is where
it boils. Negative numbers, for
example (−10°C), show
temperatures below freezing.

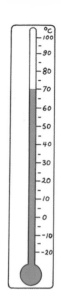

Write the temperature shown by these thermometers.

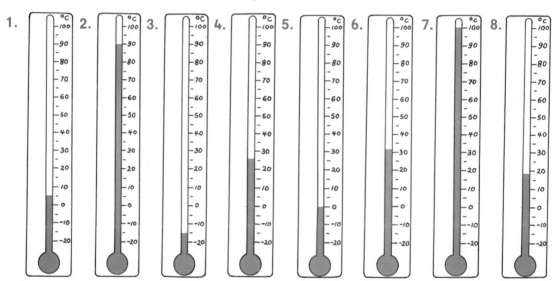

9. Put the temperatures in order from coldest to hottest.

Higher and lower temperatures

Find out the temperatures of these. You may have to ask at home
or look them up in a reference book.

10. a freezer

11. baking a cake in an oven

12. a car engine when it's running

13. the surface of Venus

One day in winter

When Wendy went to sleep
one winter's night, it was –5°C.

During the night the
temperature fell 10°C.

By noon the next day,
the temperature had
risen 20°C.

Copy and complete this chart about temperature changes.

Estimate the time of day.

	Starting temperature	Change	Temperature now	Time of day
1.	13°C	rose 7°C		
2.	8°C	rose 5°C		
3.	2°C	fell 3°C		
4.	–4°C	fell 6°C		
5.	–7°C	fell 5°C		
6.	–1°C	rose 5°C		

7. Make your own temperature chart for a day.
   Take the temperature every hour.

8. Write down the coldest and warmest time of day.

Speeds

A car which travels 40 miles in 1 hour has an average speed of 40 miles per hour (m.p.h.).

If it travels 80 miles in 2 hours it still has an average speed of 40 m.p.h. because 80 ÷ 2 = 40.

Find these average speeds and write them down.

1. 60 miles in 2 hours
2. 120 miles in 3 hours
3. 250 miles 5 hours
4. 45 miles in $1\frac{1}{2}$ hours
5. 90 miles in $2\frac{1}{2}$ hours
6. 30 miles in $\frac{1}{2}$ hour

Faster speeds

A Jumbo Jet has an average speed of about 560 m.p.h.

Concorde flies at an average speed of 1200 m.p.h.

About how long does it take each one to travel these distances?

7. 1000 miles
8. 3000 miles
9. 5000 miles
10. 500 miles

Fast animals

Many animals run, fly or swim very fast, but only for short distances. Their speeds are best measured in metres per second (m/s).

Here is a chart of the fastest runners, fliers and swimmers.

Runners		Swimmers	
Cheetah	28 m/s	Blue shark	20 m/s
Antelope	24 m/s	Sailfish	30.5 m/s
Gazelle	22 m/s	Tuna	19 m/s
Hare	20 m/s	Flying fish	15.5 m/s
Horse	19 m/s	**Fliers (level flight)**	
Greyhound	18 m/s	Swift	47.5 m/s
		Duck	29 m/s

1. Which is the fastest animal on the chart?

2. Write how far each animal on the chart can travel in 5 seconds.

3. Write how long it takes each animal in the chart to travel 100 metres.

How fast are you?

4. Measure out 10 m, 20 m, 50 m or 100 m. Time how long it takes for you and some friends to run the distance.
    Work out your average speeds in m/s.
    Make a chart.

5. Now try the same with walking.

Name	Time	Speed

Looking at parallel lines

> Remember: parallel lines never meet.
> They always stay the same distance apart.

Look at these pictures.
Which ones have parallel lines?

1.
2.
3.

4.
5.
6.

7. Draw your own picture or design showing parallel lines. Ask your friends to find all the pairs of parallel lines.

---

8. Look at the things around you in the classroom.

   Some of them have parallel lines.

   Find 6 things that have at least one pair of parallel lines.

Parallels in polygons

Draw these polygons.

Sort them into sets, those with parallel lines and those without parallel lines.

How many pairs of parallel lines does each shape have?

1.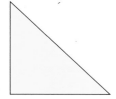
2.
3.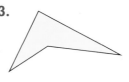
4.

5.
6.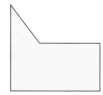
7.
8.

Draw these quadrilaterals and write their names.

9. 2 unequal pairs of parallel sides and 4 right angles

10. 1 pair of parallel sides

11. 2 pairs of parallel sides, all sides equal and 4 right angles

12. 2 pairs of parallel sides, no right angles

Some 3-D shapes have parallel lines like this cuboid.

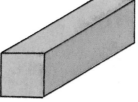

13. How many pairs of parallel lines does it have?

14. Is there another solid shape that has the same number of parallel lines?

Naming triangles

Remember:

An equilateral triangle has all sides equal

An isosceles triangle has two sides equal

A right-angled triangle has one right angle

A scalene triangle has sides of different lengths

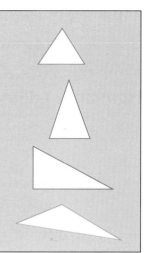

Use a ruler, a right-angle measure or a strip of card.
Name these triangles.

1.

2.

3.

4.

5.

6.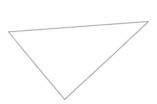

Use either square or isometric spotty paper.

7. Can you make each kind of triangle on your paper? Write the names of the ones that are easy to make.

square   or   isometric

Triangles on geoboards

You will need a square and an isometric geoboard, elastic bands and spotty paper.

1. How many different isosceles triangles can be made on a 4 x 4 square geoboard? Draw them on spotty paper.

2. How many different isosceles triangles can be made on a 4 x 4 isometric geoboard? Draw them on spotty paper.

3. How many different right-angled triangles can be made on a 4 x 4 square geoboard? Draw them on spotty paper.

4. Can right-angled triangles be constructed on an isometric geoboard?

Triangles from circles

You will need some paper circles and glue.

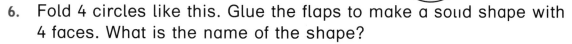

Fold the circles like this.

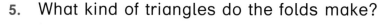

fold from any point on the circumference into the centre

fold again from one end of the first fold

fold again

5. What kind of triangles do the folds make?

6. Fold 4 circles like this. Glue the flaps to make a solid shape with 4 faces. What is the name of the shape?

7. With a friend, fold 20 circles and glue the flaps to make a solid shape with 20 faces. What is the name of this shape?

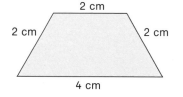

Trace the shape. Cut out 3 copies of it.

8. Put the pieces together to form a triangle.

9. What is the perimeter of the triangle?

Squares, rectangles, rulers and set squares

A set square is a drawing instrument with a right angle.

It can be used with a ruler to make clear right-angled corners when you draw squares or rectangles.

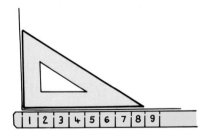

Use a ruler and set square to measure and copy these rectangles exactly on to paper.

Cut out your drawings and place them over the shapes to check how accurate they are.

1.

2.

3.

4.

6.

5.

Constructing 2-D shapes   *Unit 4*   *Drawing rectangles and squares using mathematical instruments*

Doubling up

Use a set square and a ruler to draw these squares and rectangles.
Make their sides twice as long as they are here.

1.

2.

3.
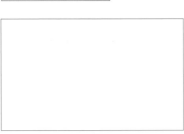

4.

Make a tangram

You will need card, a
ruler, a set square,
scissors, pencil.

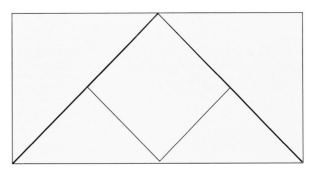

5. Measure this tangram.

   Copy it on to card and cut out the pieces.

   Use all the pieces to make each of these shapes.

   Draw them to show how the pieces fit together.

6. a square   7. a right-angled, isosceles triangle

8. a parallelogram   9. a trapezium

10. Invent your own tangram. Use a square or different rectangle
    of card.

Is it a pyramid?

triangular pyramid

square pyramid

pentagonal pyramid

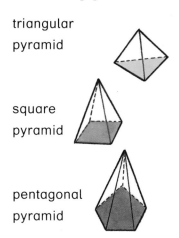

Remember: the base of a pyramid is a polygon. All the other faces are triangles which meet at a point.

Pyramids are named after their bases. The most common are square or triangular pyramids.

A regular tetrahedron is a pyramid with 4 equilateral triangular faces.

Which of these nets make pyramids?
Draw them and try to make the shapes.

1.

2.

3.

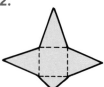

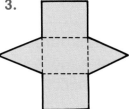

4.

5.

6.

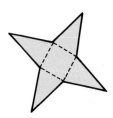

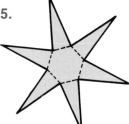

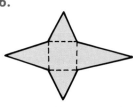

Making pyramids

This pyramid has a base 4 cm x 4 cm.
The edges of the triangular faces are
6 cm long.

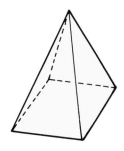

1. Draw the net for this pyramid and make it.

Make these pyramids in the same way.

2. triangular pyramid
    edges of all
    triangles 5 cm

3. square pyramid
    base 6 cm x 6 cm
    edges of
    triangles 8 cm

4. hexagonal pyramid
    edges of base 4 cm
    edges of
    triangles 7 cm

5. How many faces, edges and vertices do each of the
    pyramids have?

---

6. **Make a stellated cube**

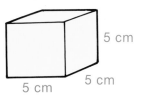

Stellated means like a star.

First make a cube 5 cm x 5 cm x 5 cm

Then make 6 square pyramids with bases
5 cm x 5 cm and edges of the triangular
faces 7 cm long.

Glue a pyramid on to each
face of the cube to make
a stellated cube.

A database – big cats

Remember: a database is a chart.

It shows information set out in 'fields'.

In this database about big cats, the fields are in the column at the side. They are 'length', 'continent', 'prey', 'colour', and so on.

Files / Fields	lion	tiger	leopard	ocelot
length	2.75 m	3 m	2.25 m	1.25 m
continent	Africa	Asia	Asia Africa	South America
main prey	wildebeest	deer	baboons deer	small mammals
colour	pale brown (tawny)	yellow and black	yellow and black	grey, fawn black
markings	none	stripes	spots	spots and stripes
habitat	plains	jungle	plains	forest and jungle
picture				

Interrogating a database

Answer these questions by using the 'big cats' database.

1. What do lions eat?

2. How long is an ocelot?

3. On which continent do tigers live?

4. What sort of markings do leopards have?

5. Which big cats do baboons avoid?

6. Which cats live on the plains?

7. Which is the longest big cat?

8. Which big cat lives in South America?

---

9. Find out more about big cats. For example, the panther, the lynx, the cheetah, and so on.

    Make your own database using the files and fields on page 120. Add any more fields you are interested in. For example, life span, number of kittens in a litter, whether they are endangered or not.

10. Do you have a hobby, collection or special interest? Design your own database. For example, if you collect stamps, you could write down the country, the currency, the prices and the pictures on them.

What do you watch?

Mr Mahmood wanted to stock his video-hire shop with tapes people liked. He asked his customers to fill in a form with the kinds of tapes they preferred.

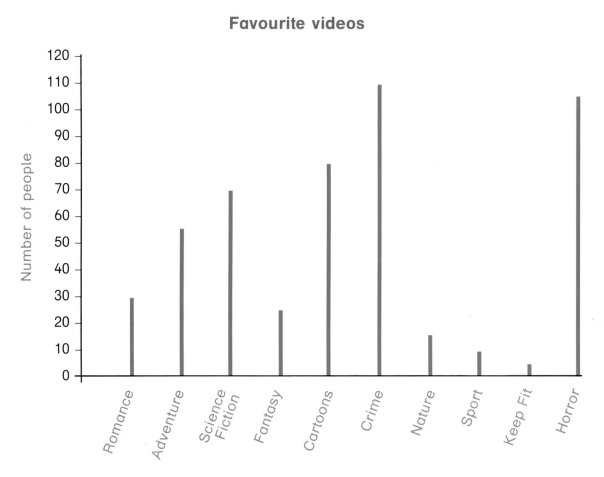

Favourite videos

1. How many people preferred adventure videos?

2. What was the most popular kind of video?

3. Which 3 videos were least popular?

4. Ask your friends about their favourite videos.

   Draw a bar line graph to show your results. What are the most and least popular?

Where can you go on holiday?

The Ross family researched holiday prices from a set of brochures to find the cheapest cost. They had lots of places in mind, so they made this list.

Cost per Person – 7 nights

Italy	£549	Belgium	£225
France	£385	Norway	£549
Spain	£479	Denmark	£399
Portugal	£535	Iceland	£329
Madeira	£379	USA	£949
Cruise	£1335	Canada	£975
Switzerland	£389	Russia	£379
Austria	£495	China	£899
Germany	£359	Caribbean	£879

1. Put these holiday prices in order from most expensive to cheapest.

2. Draw a bar-line graph to show the holiday prices.

3. If you had £400, which holiday would you choose?

4. If you had £1000, which holiday would you choose?

5. What is the most expensive holiday?

6. Where would you have to go if you had £300?

A probability scale

The chances of something happening can be shown on
a probability scale.
This is a number line from 0 to 1.

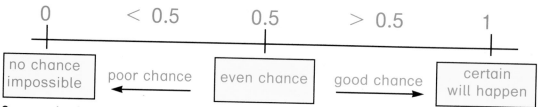

0 stands for **no chance**.

1 stands for **certain**.

0.5 is exactly between the two and stands for **even chance**.

Less than 0.5 means a **poor chance** (< 0.5)

More than 0.5 means a **good chance** (> 0.5)

Read these statements. Write 0, 1, 0.5, < 0.5 or > 0.5 to
describe the chance of them happening.

1. You will have a son one day.

2. July 3rd will be a Thursday.

3. After school today you will go home.

4. The result of tossing a coin will be tails.

5. You will go to bed tonight.

6. You will win one thousand pounds.

7. You will watch television tonight.

8. The result of throwing a dice will be six.

9. You will be nine next birthday.

10. You will go to the moon for a holiday.

11. It will snow tomorrow.

What kind of chance?

Write 0, 1, 0.5, < 0.5 or > 0.5 to answer these questions.

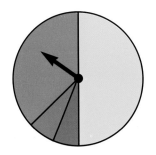

On this spinner, what are the
chances of spinning:

1. green　2. yellow　3. blue

From this bag of marbles, what are
the chances of pulling out:

4. blue　5. red　6. green

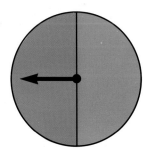

On this spinner, what are the
chances of spinning:

7. red　8. yellow　9. green

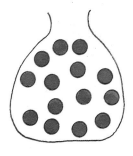

From this bag of marbles, what are
the chances of pulling out:

10. yellow　11. blue　12. red

Glossary

arc Part of the circumference of a circle.

axes The vertical and horizontal lines marked with the numbers on a grid or graph.

chord A line joining two points on the circumference of a circle.

circumference The perimeter of a circle.

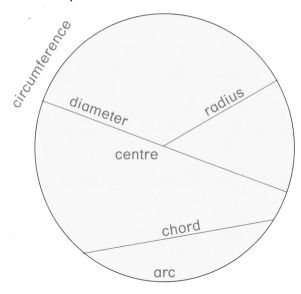

co-ordinates Numbers used to show position on a chart or grid.

congruent shapes Identical shapes.

diameter A straight line from the circumference of a circle, through the centre and to the opposite point on the circumference.

digit 0, 1, 2, 3, 4, 5, 6, 7, 8, 9 are the digits. The numeral 346, is made from the digits 3, 4 and 6.

equivalent fractions Fractions that have the same value. $\frac{1}{2}, \frac{2}{4}, \frac{3}{6}, \frac{5}{10}$ are equivalent fractions.

expanded form A way of writing out a numeral to show the value of each of its digits. $7000 + 500 + 20 + 1$ is the expanded form of 7521.

factor A factor of a number is a number that will divide exactly into that number. 1, 2, 4 and 8 are all factors of 8.

function A combination of operations and numbers, for example, (x 3) or (+ 5 − 2).

horizontal A line parallel to the ground or, when represented on a sheet of paper, parallel to the bottom and top edges.

inverse operations Operations which can 'undo' each other, such as, addition and subtraction ($6 + 2 = 8$; $8 − 2 = 6$) and multiplication and division ($2 \times 3 = 6$; $6 \div 3 = 2$).

isosceles triangle A triangle with two equal sides.

mean The mean of a set of data is found by adding the data and dividing the total by the number of data. The mean of 2, 5 and 5 is $12 \div 3 = 4$.

median The middle number or measurement when a set of data is put in order. The median of 2, 4, 7, 9, 12, 56, 72 is 9. If there is an even number of data it is the mean of the two middle numbers or measures.

mode The number, measurement or item which appears most often in a set of data. The mode of 6 cm, 5 cm, 6 cm, 2 cm, 6 cm is 6 cm.

multiple A multiple of a number is produced by multiplying that number by another number. 3, 6 and 9 are multiples of 3.

ordered pair A pair of numbers used for showing position on a chart or grid. (6, 2) is an ordered pair. Each number is a co-ordinate.

parallel lines Straight lines that are always the same distance apart and never meet.

perimeter The distance all the way round a shape.

probability The likelihood of something happening.

polygon A closed 2-D shape made from straight lines.

pyramid A 3-D shape with a polygon as a base and whose other faces are triangles all meeting at a point.

radius A line drawn from the centre of a circle to the circumference.

range The difference between the greatest and the least in a set of data. The range of 4, 2, 7, 20, 13 is $20 - 2 = 18$.

regular polygon A polygon whose sides and angles are equal.

scalene triangle A triangle in which all the sides (and angles) are unequal.

square number The result of multiplying a number by itself. 4, 9, 16, 25, 100 are square numbers.

square root The square root of a number is the number that when multiplied by itself will give that number. The square root of 4 is 2 (because 2 x 2 = 4).

vertical A line perpendicular to the ground. When represented on paper, a line parallel to the sides of the paper.